LET'S PUT ON
A SHOW!

Theatre Production for Novices

Stewart F. L

HEINEMANN
Portsmouth, NH

Heinemann
A division of Reed Elsevier Inc.
361 Hanover Street
Portsmouth, NH 03801–3912
www.heinemanndrama.com

Offices and agents throughout the world

Library of Congress Cataloging-in-Publication Data
Lane, Stewart F.
  Let's put on a show! : theatre production for novices / Stewart F. Lane.
    p. cm.
  Includes index.
  ISBN-13: 978-0-325-00981-0
  ISBN-10: 0-325-00981-3
  1. Theater—Production and direction.   I. Title.

PN2053.L35 2007
792.02'32—dc22   2007006269

Editors: Lisa A. Barnett *and* Cheryl Kimball
Production management: Denise A. Botelho
Production coordination: Vicki Kasabian
Cover design: Joni Doherty Design
Author photo: Roy Weinstein
Typesetter: Val Levy / Drawing Board Studios
Manufacturing: Steve Bernier

Printed in the United States of America on acid-free paper
11   10   09   08   VP   2   3   4   5

Contents

Acknowledgments

I would like to dedicate this book to all those foolish enough to fall in love with the theatre. I'd also like to make a special dedication to my wife, Bonnie, for her constant support.

Thank you also to Howard Meyer, director and playwright at the Axial Theatre Company in Pleasantville, New York; Terry Bortom, director of The American Magic-Lantern Theater and my friend Glenn Young, professor of playwriting and founding publisher of Applause Books, Rich Mintzer, and Liz Lewis for their contributions. Also, thank you to John Kenrick of Musicals101.com for his help.

I would also wish to thank my father for teaching me business and Jimmy Nederlander for teaching me the business of theatre. They are not always the same thing.

Introduction

My love affair with the theatre began when I was invited to see my first Broadway show. I was eleven at the time, and the father of my best friend, Ricky, was an actor. I had never heard of him so I didn't think much about it (except it was kind of cool that he worked at night, when it was fun, and not like everyone else who worked during the day). The ritual of putting on my only suit, getting a haircut, and keeping my nails clean all added to the feeling that something special was about to happen.

We drove from Long Island into the City, which was an exciting event in itself. Everything kept snowballing from there: seeing my first beautiful Broadway theatre, getting a ticket with the name of the show printed on it (instead of the usual "Admit One" that you'd get at the movie houses), being handed a Playbill (two souvenirs and the curtain wasn't even up yet!), and quickly being ushered into the first row in front of a huge, plush crimson curtain. The overture began and my mouth dropped open. The curtain rose and my eyes popped at what they saw. Indeed, Ricky's father, Sid Caesar, was starring in the musical *Little Me*, music by Cy Coleman, lyrics by Carolyn Leigh, and book by Neil Simon. The audience roared with laughter and, because we were in the front row, I could see some behind-the-scenes preparation by the actors in the wings. I was now an insider (and after only five minutes). Afterward we went backstage, where Sid was holding court. There were many well-wishers and plenty of backslapping and hugging going on. So much laughter onstage and off, I thought. With a refrigerator, bed, TV, and hot plate, this place was like a home away from home. My heavens, why would anyone want to do anything else?

And so it began, my marriage to the theatre. I started joining every drama club and taking every acting class I could, both in school and in town. In the ninth grade, I was in my first show, *Harvey*, in which I played the cab driver. My character did not come on stage until the very end of the show, in the final five minutes. To this day, I don't know if it was my brilliant performance or if everybody was simply waiting for me to show up so they would know the show would be over soon, but as soon as I came out onstage the entire audience stood up and applauded. I couldn't have hoped for a better start to my acting career.

I went on to Boston University, where I majored in theatre and acting and from which I would receive my BFA. More recently, I was honored to be named a distinguished alumnus of both the College of Fine Arts and Boston University itself. Along with the classical training I received at BU, I also ventured out to do summer stock in Monticello and other venues throughout upstate New York (otherwise known as the Catskills), where I got my education in musicals while performing in shows like George and Ira Gershwin's *Girl Crazy,* Gilbert and Sullivan's *HMS Pinafore* and Cole Porter's *Anything Goes.*

Along with performing, I took various jobs in the industry. One summer, I worked as an assistant to a casting director for movies, which included popular titles like *The Exorcist* and *Cops and Robbers.* At another time, I worked as an apprentice at the New Jersey Shakespeare Festival, watching the actors and saying to myself, "I can do this stuff!" You have to have a certain amount of ego and believe in yourself to be an actor. While I wouldn't call myself a "dancer," I moved well onstage, and although I also was not a "belter," I could carry a tune. And I enjoyed acting immensely.

I wanted very much to get my equity card, and at the end of the Shakespeare Festival, the general manager told me that he knew how I could get my card. He had a friend who ran a theatre in Sullivan, Illinois, and was looking to extend the summer season into the fall. However, he needed people to help out. He told a few of us that he could hire us and we would get equity contracts if we could go and help him run his theatre, as well as perform. So, along with two other compatriots, I spent September through Thanksgiving working on shows at The Little Theater on the Square in Sullivan, Illinois. This included many technical jobs that I had learned over the years in school, such as set building and hanging lights. Of course, we also performed in the show and received our equity cards. Then it was back to New York to do some modeling, film work, television, and touring with former screen star Van Johnson and the "Voice of Kraft," Ed Herlihy.

From there it was off to Los Angeles, where I was determined to forge ahead with my acting pursuits. However, after a year out West, I grew homesick for New York City. I had seen the lights on

Broadway and missed them terribly. Theatre takes a backseat to everything in LA, where film, television, and the recording industry reign. I returned to New York and took stock of my situation. I realized that I loved the theatre and being part of the business, but that I had to come up with a better approach if I was going to succeed. So Jimmy Nederlander (whom I had worked for as a script reader) offered me a job as the assistant house manager at the Brooks Atkinson Theater during the last several months of *Same Time, Next* Year, by Bernard Slade. Now, instead of dealing with plot, character, and motivation, I found myself dealing with patrons, tickets, boilers, and the box office. It was at the Brooks Atkinson Theater that I would become an assistant producer and later move into my career as a producer.

Now, more than thirty years later, and having been fortunate enough to win three Antoine Perry Awards (a/k/a Tonys) and enjoyed producing several successful Broadway musicals—including *La Cage aux Folles, Woman of the Year, The Will Rogers Follies,* and *Thoroughly Modern Millie*, I can truly say my marriage to the theatre—AND TO PRODUCING—has been a hit.

Of course, falling in love is easy, but making a marriage work takes discipline, patience, and understanding. Producing is much the same. That is what prompted me to write this book. I wanted you all to share not only in the exciting experience and camaraderie of the theatre, but in what it takes to put together a show—including the hard work and dedication involved.

I did not set out to write a textbook for drama students, but rather to inject some of my own personal accounts into what I hope serves as an entertaining "how-to" guide for anyone putting on a show, at any level. I consider it Theatre for Non–Theatre Majors, a broad overview of the process behind staging a show. In some cases you may serve as the producer, while in other situations, you will find yourself also taking on the role of director. In amateur productions, particularly in schools and universities, I always found that wearing several hats and pitching in and helping in various capacities were valuable learning experiences. Therefore, you will see some crossover throughout the book, explaining jobs that are handled by producers or directors. Only at the professional level—and when actors are union members—will you see roles more carefully defined. Having directed, written, and performed in shows, and having worked in various other behind-the-scenes capacities, I have learned that a knowledge of all aspects of a production will serve you well.

Within the following nine chapters, you will get a taste of what it takes to put a show together. Before embarking on the actual process, I ask the basic [musical] question; Why put on a show? Once you have established your reason, whether to help actors hone their craft or to raise money for a good cause, it is time to select a show that meets your needs, one you believe in and for which you have a vision. Then, before seeking your creative team or staging auditions, I present a few of the many organizational and technical issues you will need to consider, including putting your budget together, finding a rehearsal space, and if necessary, locating a theatre.

Auditions, casting, rehearsals, and how to publicize your show are also discussed, with some key points plus a few tricks of the trade included. In Chapter 10, we divert to playwriting, a lengthy subject presented in a very abbreviated form. Throughout the book, you will encounter Tales from the Trenches as an entertaining reminder that, in live theatre, you should always expect the unexpected.

So, if you're ready . . . LET'S PUT ON A SHOW!

Why Put On a Show?

Sometimes you have an experience that reminds you why you enjoy the business of putting on a show. In the mid-1990s, I was asked to produce Liza Minnelli's show, *Minnelli on Minnelli* at The Palace Theater on Broadway. I was kind of excited about it because of the historical connection between the Minnelli family and the Palace Theater. It was at the Palace that Judy Garland had her brilliant Broadway debut, plus, of course, her comeback in the late 1960s. So for Liza, it would be a marvelous place to stage a comeback after her battles with drugs and other personal problems. It was potentially a very big event, but I was also worried about it and expressed my concerns to her manager about whether she was ready for such a comeback show.

Then one day I got a phone call. It was Liza. She invited me up to her apartment for what I assumed would be a discussion of the possible show. Well, she treated me like visiting royalty, giving me the grand tour, which included showing me wonderful paintings of her father that Andy Warhol had done.

Now, I thought, we'll sit down and talk business, but it wasn't to be. Instead, Liza Minnelli proceeded to sing for me—

the entire show, right there in her living room. Talk about your command performance. It was amazing, and I was totally overwhelmed by her talent, her sincerity, and her efforts to make this dream come true. I was completely won over and went on to produce *Minnelli on Minnelli* at the Palace Theater . . . and she was absolutely brilliant.

Theatre has always been uniquely designed to explore the human condition. The immediacy and, in some cases, the intimacy of a theatrical production can leave a lasting impression on an audience. Breathing life into the theatrical work, which, in this case, means staging the production, is a very gratifying experience to those involved.

Theatre also typically draws together a diverse cross-section of talented individuals who bond for the good of the big picture, which is the show. For everyone involved in a production, the challenge of staging a show usually serves as a tremendous learning experience. The concept of teamwork, the use of critical thinking, and the need to be responsible, as well as accountable, for completing the numerous tasks intrinsic to the full production provide valuable life lessons. In addition, working on a show is a great way to become an active part of the community. In fact, theatre has long been a means of communicating the fears, dreams, or desires of a community or a segment within the larger community. Modern-day theatre emerged from the church during the Renaissance. As a result, churches and synagogues are still a cornerstone of theatre in communities throughout the country and around the world.

From a practical perspective, a theatrical production can be a marvelous way to raise money for a cause or an institution. While selling wrapping paper, magazine subscriptions, cookies, or candy bars takes far less effort, staging a show presents many more possibilities for everyone involved. Grade schools, middle schools and high schools, universities, social organizations, associations, religious groups, charities, and even businesses have all taken to the stage to deliver a message and raise funds. What makes this a particularly enjoyable and fulfilling means of fundraising is the collaborative experience.

Theatre is people oriented; it is one of the most collaborative industries you will ever find. Whether you are creating a new play or doing a revival, the interaction between the people involved in lighting, set design, costumes, publicity, and all the many aspects of the production is a marvelous experience—it's like building a house. The culmination of the effort that it takes to put on a show is hard to duplicate, especially because so many different skills and talents are necessary. From choreography to carpentry to technological expertise, there are jobs to be done that tap into a wide range of skills and abilities.

Socializing and camaraderie are also fundamental aspects of the theatre. Lasting friendships are not uncommon. While interning at the New Jersey Shakespeare Festival in 1974, I met a fellow up-and-coming actor. Like me, as he grew older, got married, and had kids, his priorities changed. The excitement of going to the Alabama Shakespeare Festival or the Alaskan Repertory Theater became less and less attractive. Like me, my friend gave up acting. While I went into producing plays, he went into producing buildings as part of the construction company owned by his wife's side of the family. We remained friends over the years and he worked his way up to president of the company. But it is hard to rid oneself of the acting bug. In fact, he told me that in another ten years he's thinking of going back to acting. Having built up a substantial nest egg, he now gives three primary reasons why it would be easier the second time around. "Number one, it's always easier to get the part when you don't really need it. Number two, there's less competition at my age, and number three, I'd have plenty of time to devote to it." He added that perhaps we could start the Old Farts Repertory Theater.

You may also meet many people that you will touch base with periodically over the years. For example, Alfre Woodard, a regular on the hit series *Desperate Housewives*, attended Boston University at the same time as I did. She has gone on to appear in more than seventy motion pictures and television appearences and received the Independent Spirit Award for her role as Chantelle in the 1992 film *Passion Fish*. She also received an Oscar nomination for best supporting actress for her role of Geechee in the 1983 release *Cross Creek*. We were in the same school of drama on our way to earning bachelor of fine arts degrees. Today we stay in touch, sometimes meeting for dinner when she comes to town. There's a bond among theatre people that can last forever.

Honing Skills

From a professional perspective, discovering new skills or enhancing your current abilities are also good reasons for becoming involved in a show. Community theatre has long been a place where lawyers, salespersons, teachers, and even doctors have improved upon their ability to speak in public. It may also serve as a place where the nine-to-fiver can utilize skills not often utilized in a board room; there is rarely a need to launch into a Gershwin tune during a stockholders' meeting.

For newcomers in any number of fields, theatre productions, whether in a school, church, or community-group setting, can serve as a training ground. Budding young artists can have their work seen when designing sets, while a craftsperson or carpenter can show off his or her skills by building the set. Theatre provides a wealth of opportunities for individuals to utilize their skills. Many leading theatrical publicists and marketing professionals started out by promoting and marketing shows that were being staged at the universities they were attending.

Actors in regional theatre companies benefit from each and every performance. These groups provide the dedicated performer with the opportunity to hone his or her present skills and acquire new ones. In one season, a diverse program of comedies and dramatic pieces can provide a comedic actor with a venue to test his or her ability to handle serious and humorous roles. Young playwrights also benefit from such theatre companies by having the opportunity to have their work showcased in the proper forum. Hearing and seeing a piece performed is of enormous value to the playwright and can push regular players in the company to work harder to create and communicate a work that is completely new and original.

Making a Statement

The theatre can be a powerful tool when a group, organization, or individual has a message to deliver. For centuries, theatre has been a forum for raising public awareness at all levels and for numerous issues. Plays about personal freedoms, such as Howard Sackler's *The*

Great White Hope, or an antiwar message in a play such as Bertolt Brecht's *Mother Courage*, present strong messages.

Parent groups and various organizations have staged plays in schools to illustrate the dangers of drug and alcohol abuse. In the early 1960s, a New York City adoption support group used an original play to educate prospective parents about the manner in which the adoption process worked in the United States at that time. Ex–Monty Python member, John Cleese produced a whole series of skits for IBM to teach business people new ways to back up important data. Problems of social significance found in corporate America, such as sexual harassment in the workplace, have also been illustrated via the use of one-act plays. Whether through a play about the HIV virus, such as Larry Kramer's *The Normal Heart*, or about failing marriages, gay marriage, or spousal or child abuse, theatre can amplify the concerns of a community and educate people. Within the prison community, theatre is helpful for rehabilitation purposes.

Of course, not all theatre is designed to make a bold statement. Theatre can also be primarily for the purpose of entertainment. High school teachers putting on a performance of Abe Burrows' classic *Guys and Dolls* for their students to forge a greater student-teacher bond, or a play staged to bolster morale and entertain American soldiers overseas are also serving a valuable purpose, even though the shows themselves are lighthearted.

Many children's theatre ensembles provide entertainment as well as education for youngsters. Students of all ages are both invigorated and impacted by exposure to theatre arts.

Fundraising: "It's More Than Just Selling Tickets"

Several thousand theatrical productions are staged annually for the purpose of fundraising. Some are for a charitable cause while others raise money to sustain a theatre company or keep the theatre program running. While saying, "Let's put on a show" is one of the easiest ways to motivate a group of people, it is also a far more loaded statement than it might appear. Simply put, it is not all that simple.

Before launching a fundraising production, it is crucial that you sit down with someone who is good at punching up numbers and determine exactly how much you are looking to raise, particularly if you need to cover the expenses of your proposed show.

In either case, whether staging a nonprofit or for-profit production, put together a budget outlining the costs. Leave no stone unturned. How much is the lumber going to cost to build the sets? How much can you spend on plants for the Howard Ashman-Alan Menken musical *The Little Shop of Horrors* (don't buy real ones, they'll die on you)? Can you really afford a full roller-skating track for your production of Andrew Lloyd Webber's *Starlight Express*? Do your best to create a realistic, accurate budget, one that, with a dedicated fundraising effort, you could actually cover. Remember, shows can range from bold extravaganzas to one-person monologues with no sets and no props. Most likely, your production will fall somewhere in that vast range in between. Even before selecting a show, have an idea of the money you can afford to spend. Look for ways to cut corners. For example, see what props and costumes the cast and crew members may have sitting in their closets or attics that might be useful. The creative juices of your ensemble can be very helpful and even beneficial. Remember, ingenuity is a zero-cost budget item.

Most school or amateur productions have low budgets, spending money only on a simple set and a few key props, some of which are rented. You should not need to pay for labor since the cast and crew is readily available. Often schools have an inventory of costumes used in previous productions that you can browse through, and alter if necessary, to meet your needs. Go through the wardrobe department if there is one and think creatively. Remember, with some safety pins, Belle's apron from Disney's *Beauty and the Beast* is Golda's *sheitel* (kerchief) in Joseph Stein, Sheldon Harnick, and Jerry Bock's *Fiddler on the Roof.*

One expense that is always necessary is paying for the rights to the show, unless the playwright is among your cast or crew members. Samuel French, Inc., has been providing the rights to published plays for 175 years and has a massive selection of titles available. Typically you will pay a fee for one performance and an additional fee for each subsequent performance. For example, Bernard Slade's *Same Time, Next Year* will cost you $50 for one night rights and $40 for each night thereafter. Neil Simon's *Barefoot in the Park* will cost $75 for each show, first to last. Musicals generally cost a little more, with an additional, small fee for the music. You can visit Samuel French online at www.samuelfrench.com and browse their show listings. They are one of several licensing and publishing houses with numerous plays available.

If you are in a position to be funded by your organization, school, or a generous grant, you will be limited by the amount of money provided. While you will not have to raise money to cover the staging of the show, you will still need a budget to stay within the financial parameters. You should then set financial goals (how much money you hope to raise for your cause) and work hard to achieve them.

In some fundraising situations, you are looking to raise a certain amount for a specific purpose. For example, you may be looking to raise money to renovate the school cafeteria. After consulting with the school administrators and getting an estimate of the cost of the renovations from professional contractors, shoot for that specific number as your fundraising goal. For example, if it would cost $5,000 to renovate the cafeteria, you have your fundraising goal in sight.

The most obvious means of raising money is through ticket sales. Your pricing will depend on several factors, including

- your costs, should you need to cover expenses,
- the size of your venue and number of available seats,
- the number of productions you plan to stage,
- the length of the performance,
- the demographics of your audience,
- your reputation of the performers or the reputation of your school, church/synagogue, association, etc., and
- anything else included with the cost of admission (i.e., you can cover your printing bill for the programs by adding $.50 or $1 to the price of each ticket).

Other Methods of Fundraising

While packing the house for every performance may be the dream of every producer, there are other ways to profit from producing a show. Whether you are staging a musical on Broadway or a drama in your local community center, some retailers in your surrounding neighborhood will want to advertise their goods or services to your audience. Sponsorship and ad sales are a time-tested means of raising funds; in fact, sponsorship has become increasingly common in modern-day theatre. Recently, Hilton Hotels and Resorts sponsored the Broadway revival of Ian Fleming's *Chitty Chitty Bang Bang* at the Hilton Theatre, while Visa sponsored the national tour of the Billy Joel, Twyla Tharp musical *Movin' Out*. Appropriately enough, Hormel Foods, the makers of Spam, were sponsors of Monty Python's comedic Broadway musical *Spamalot*.

Prior to approaching potential sponsors or advertisers, have all the details of your show in hand, including the date and times of each performance, the venue, and the seating capacity. You need to be up front with potential sponsors regarding the gist of the play; don't tell people it's a musical comedy and then come in with Arthur Miller's *Death of a Salesman*. Also, while promoting the show to sponsors, as well as to your audience, make sure to clearly define the show. When I was in school, we put on a production of George S. Kaufman and Moss Hart's *The Man Who Came to Dinner*, in which a literary critic breaks his hip and happens to be in a wheelchair throughout the show, which is the basis for high comedy in the play. The promotion for the show was a picture of a man in a wheelchair. It looked like an ad asking people to donate to muscular dystrophy (which in itself is not a bad thing, but it won't sell tickets to the show)—or at least an ad for a far more serious, dramatic play. The point is, you need to carefully evaluate the materials you are using to promote the play (including your sales pitch), whether to local businesses or to the general public.

While sponsors and advertisers need to know the type of play they are putting their money behind, you also need to use some discretion when seeking support. As hard as it may be to turn them down, you may not want Seagram's Whiskey or the Pink Pussycat Boutique sponsoring your fourth-grade production of James Barrie's classic, *Peter Pan*.

In some cases, you can try seeking out the most appropriate sponsor for a show. If, for example, your show is promoting safe sex, you might look for a condom manufacturer as a sponsor. And who better than a hairspray manufacturer to sponsor your rendition of Marc Shaiman's *Hairspray*? Use creative thinking along those lines. Be prepared ahead of time to work a little harder when it comes to selling advertising and sponsorship for a more controversial show, such as Jerome Lawrence and Robert F. Lee's *Inherit the Wind*, which talks about the evolution of man, intelligence, and creative and intellectual design, topics that have always sparked discussion.

For advertising purposes, you also need to be prepared with the details of what it is you are selling. How much advertising space do you have available? Where will ads be placed? The program will need to be roughed out ahead of time so you will have an idea of how many pages you have to sell. Posters, window cards, and even the actual tickets are also potential places for advertisers or sponsors to catch the eye of your audience and promote their products or services. In some cases, you might even hand out product samples with the program. There are numerous possibilities. Plan in advance where sponsors can display their companies. But make sure your production is not overwhelmed by advertising.

Remember to enhance your ad sales and sponsorship possibilities by having a few choice seats set aside for sponsors. Make them feel special and they may be back again sponsoring your next production. By involving the local community in one production, you open the door for future sponsorship. Once a local business agrees to place an ad in your program or sponsor the printing of two thousand tickets, other businesses will see the opportunity to reach prospective customers in the same manner. Or the business can help you promote your show simply by placing a sign in a shop window or a poster in a business office.

It is also imperative that before going out in an effort to raise funds, you have a system set up so someone involved with the show can manage all incoming monies and answer questions from prospective advertisers or sponsors. Many times, the producer is too busy to handle the sponsorship and advertising responsibilities for a show, so a committee is formed to handle such responsibilities. One person should handle, and keep track of, all incoming funds.

Patrons of the Arts

Along with businesses, individuals have long served as sponsors in the theatre community. Patrons of the arts, as they are known, are those generous benefactors who appreciate the influence, impact, and significance the theatre has brought to the community at large. As far back as the early 1900s, some of New York's wealthiest families,

Product placement is simply receiving payment for placing the actual product, the product name, or even the logo in the show. When Frank Loesser and Abe Burrow's *How to Succeed in Business Without Really Trying* returned to Broadway in the mid-1990s, the show incorporated an Eight O'Clock Coffee blimp onstage. It was totally different from the original production, and the audiences loved it. In Neil Simon and Cy Coleman's latest revival of *Sweet Charity*, tequila maker Jose Cuervo's Gran Centenario was mentioned in the script, the line change being okayed by Mr. Simon himself. Product placement is found not only on Broadway. In Louisville, Kentucky, a production of the Richard Maltby Jr. and Murray Horwitz revue *Ain't Misbehavin'* included onstage table lamps made from Jack Daniels bottles.

While the concept of receiving payment for using name brands is growing, mentioning products onstage is not entirely new. In a manner of speaking, name brands have been featured in theatre for years without anyone paying a price. Song lyrics such as "I would give up a coffee for a Sanka" from the song "Bianca," by Cole Porter, in Samuel and Bella Spewack's *Kiss Me, Kate*; "I could say, life is just a bowl of Jell-O" from "A Cockeyed Optimist" in Rodgers and Hammerstein's *South Pacific*, or "We import the drinks that you buy, so your Perrier is Canada Dry" from the title tune in Jerry Herman and Harvey Fierstein's *La Cage aux Folles* are one way in which product names have made their way onto the stage in a most unobtrusive manner.

Think about where a product can fit into the show for your purposes without altering the dialogue or detracting from the scene. For example, if a character is taking a trip and calls a travel agent, have the stickers of a local travel agency on the luggage. The menus that a couple are reading from during a restaurant scene could be from a local eatery. In *Thoroughly Modern Millie*, book by Richard Morris, and lyrics by Dick Scanlon, music by Jeanine Tesori, which takes place in the 1920s, we used a Van Husen shirt ad as a backdrop because the shirts and ads were very popular at that time.

Of course, subtlety is paramount when using product placement. The stage production of the hit motion picture *Big*, book by John Weidman, was an example of how product placement can backfire, even when it is intrinsic to the story line. In the film, the well-known toy store FAO Schwarz was featured, particularly when Tom Hanks sidestepped his way joyfully across the large on-floor piano keys. In the stage version, however, having prominently dis-playing FAO Schwarz came across as crass and too commercial. You need to make sure that product placement respects the fine line between subtlety and blatant commercialism.

Once You Know Why, Everything Else Follows

Knowing why you are putting on a show will open the door for all that will follow. Whether fundraising or inspirational, your goal for staging a show can be the motivation that draws your performers and crew and beckons your community to get involved, whether it is a university, religious group, or the neighborhood.

Your reasons for staging a show will directly affect your choice of show and how it will be marketed and promoted. A theatre en-semble doing four or five shows in a season will want to promote the benefits of theatre in general and the need to support the arts in the community, while a fundraiser to save a local landmark will promote the show in conjunction with the need to embrace the town's history. If the goal is to teach youngsters the dangers of abusing alcohol, the marketing will take a different approach. In each case, it is through the theatre that you will communicate your message. In the next chapter, we look at the significance of select-ing the right show for your purposes.

Selecting a Show

Frankenstein, I thought. Why not a hit Broadway version of this classic Mary Shelley story? It was January 4, 1981, when my full-blown production of *Frankenstein* opened at the Palace Theater on Broadway. It was also January 4, 1981, when it closed, giving it the dubious honor of becoming the most expensive nonmusical ever to open and close in one night. The real honor, came when my name was added to the wall at Joe Allen's in Manhattan. A hangout for theatregoers early in the evening and theatre people—actors, directors, producers, and crew members—after the shows close, Joe Allen's had created a special wall of immortality. Unlike the other bars and restaurants that hail the many hits on Broadway, Joe Allen's dedicates their wall to framed posters of Broadway's biggest flops. Hal Prince, David Merrick, and, yes, Stewart Lane are on the wall. It's a badge of honor and a testament to the fact that along the way every producer has some flops; it's simply part of the business, paying your dues. They can't all be hits, and you've got to roll with the punches . . . which is also a good metaphor for life.

Few elementary school classes stage Eugene O'Neill's *The Iceman Cometh*, and probably fewer church groups have staged Richard O'Brien's *The Rocky Horror Picture Show*. While classics like Lionel Bart's *Oliver!* (from Dickens' classic *Oliver Twist*) and Thomas Meehan's *Annie* (from Harold Gray's classic comic strip "Little Orphan Annie") work well as elementary school fundraisers, *Mother Courage* is for a completely different audience. Your choice of show will be influenced by numerous factors, including how much time and effort you can devote to the project. Are you bold enough to stage a production by an as-yet-undiscovered playwright or are you more comfortable with a classic Gilbert and Sullivan? Ibsen or Neil Simon? Tennessee Williams or Andrew Lloyd Webber? So many choices and so many factors to consider.

In this chapter we look at the process of narrowing down a wealth of possibilities and selecting a show that is right for your target audience, fits your budget, is suitable for your prospective cast, meets your goals (as discussed in Chapter 1) and meets the approval of those in power positions, be they the school board or your financial backers.

Therefore, before making the posters and printing the tickets, you need to carefully select a show that meets your many needs.

Size Matters

How many performers do you have? The size of your group is an integral part of determining an appropriate show. A repertory theatre company can limit the number of players or add new cast members according to which shows the theatre company wants to put on in a given season. Members of an association, corporation, or religious group, on the other hand, may base their decision on the budget and space available first then hold auditions for the roles. In schools, it is often a matter of trying to include everyone in the class, or drama department, in some manner, whether onstage or backstage. If, for example, you have a large drama department and want to showcase a lot of your performers, you might choose something like *The Man Who Came to Dinner*, which has a large cast. In an all-girls school you might want to consider doing *Annie* and bringing in a couple of male faculty members to play the two male roles.

In the theatre, there are almost always creative means of solving problems. For example, I once did a high school production of Arthur Miller's *The Crucible* on two nights. We had two excellent performers for the female lead, so I gave the role to each of them for one performance. You can even split large classes into two entirely separate casts, one for Monday's show and one for Tuesday's performance. For a grade school, you might consider what the teachers at an elementary school in Westchester, New York, did. Knowing that they had nearly fifty students to include from their three fifth-grade classes and how difficult Shakespeare was to learn, they divided *A Midsummer Night's Dream* up and had each class perform one act. The show worked very well, and none of the youngsters had to struggle by learning too many lines from the Immortal Bard.

For younger students, the difficulty and number amount of lines as well the content of the play are relevant factors in making your selection. Choose a show that holds the students' interest, has a positive message, and is simple enough to learn. With that in mind, many teachers have found themselves making abbreviated versions of classic shows. Freddie Gershon, a theatrical producer of numerous films and musicals throughout the 1970s, '80s and '90s, also recognized the need for abbreviated shows. Gershon, who is chairman and CEO of Musical Theatre International (MTI), one of the world's foremost (and oldest) licensing companies, realized that thanks to computer games, videos, and similar diversions, children's attention spans were getting increasingly shorter and that it was a struggle for them to handle a two-hour production. He took a look at the extensive MTI catalog, which includes classics like *West Side Story, Annie, Guys and Dolls, Fiddler on the Roof*, and decided to develop the Broadway Junior Program. He legitimized "abbreviated" versions of musicals by creating seventy-minute formats, that uphold the story line, include the most popular musical numbers, and provide young children with workable productions. You can check out the large selection of shows included in MTI's Broadway Jr. Program at www.mtimusicalworlds.com.

Another significant size issue you may face when determining which show is best for your needs, is that of the physical space. Let's face it: If you are working in a small venue with limited stage space—often referred to as a black box theatre—it is unlikely you will be able to put on a production of Rodgers and Hammerstein's

Oklahoma! or any musical with large dance numbers. Nor will you see much scenery flying around. Again, this is where creativity can factor into your plans. One of the most innovative uses of space I ever saw was a staged production of *Mother Courage* staged in a garage by The Performing Garage Theater Company. Because there was little actual performance space, they moved the audience to different parts of the garage where they would do scenes. At one point, they opened the garage doors and performed on the streets of New York—in January. I'll never forget watching a scene of this powerful play being done as a police patrol car drove by.

At Yale University, in 1974, the drama department used the on-campus swimming pool for their performances of Burt Shevelove's musical adaptation of *The Frogs*, a show originally written in 405 B.C. by Aristophanes, with music by the far more contemporary Stephen Sondheim. Since most often you will have few choices, and possibly actors who can't swim, you will likely be limited to an available stage. One of the producer's challenges is to make the show fit the stage—within reason, of course. A creative ensemble can make the job a lot easier.

Stage size notwithstanding, consider the size of your rehearsal space. Just because you have a large stage and six months to learn, rehearse, and stage *Oklahoma!* does not mean you will have a facility in which to rehearse it. It is not uncommon for the theatre or auditorium where you will hold your production to be booked or unavailable for your rehearsals. So consider your rehearsal possibilities before making a show selection. A small show, such as Neil Simon's *Barefoot in the Park* (five actors, one set), can be rehearsed in someone's living room if necessary. However, rehearsing the Jerome Kern and Oscar Hammerstein musical *Showboat* will require a much larger space than a standard, or even an exceptionally large, living room.

The length of time in which you have to put together a production can be another major factor in your choice of show. If your schedule is open-ended, meaning you can set any date you choose, well in advance, then this is not an issue. However, in most cases, such as trying to raise money for a specific cause, filling a schedule for your theatre company, or having only three months until the end of the semester, you will not have the luxury of an open-ended timetable. Therefore, you will want to factor in the learning curve of each show.

In general, a full-blown musical with a cast of twenty-five is far more difficult to stage than a dramatic play with a cast of six. In addition, some shows present more complicated material than others. Considering that you will need to schedule rehearsals around everything else that takes place in your school, church, temple, community center, or other space, you will want to select a show that can actually be learned and rehearsed in the time frame you are given. Of course, a trained theatre ensemble will have a much easier time learning a show in six weeks than a third-grade class will.

Remember Why You Are Staging a Show

Once you decide why you are staging your show (see Chapter 1), you will need to attract an audience. Revivals of popular shows typically draw more interest from the public at large than a brand-new, original play. As a general rule, people are reluctant to buy tickets to an unfamiliar show. If you are looking to raise money, go with a show that would appeal to a wide audience. Repertory companies that put on several productions will often open their season with a revival of a popular Broadway hit to secure some funding for the remainder of the season (and generate positive reviews) before moving on to more obscure or original plays.

Selling tickets to a show is another marketing factor; therefore, you need to know your demographics. Who are most likely to buy tickets? Consider the age range, size of the community, and makeup of the group. Are you selling tickets only to students on campus? Are you selling to the community at large? Are most of your buyers families? Is your audience primarily made up of a particular ethnic heritage? Are you reaching out to a large gay and lesbian population? Not that you want to pander to a specific group, but you do want to enhance your chances of selling tickets by presenting a production that is likely to appeal to a specific demographic group. You also do not want to put on a show which is likely to bore your audience or possibly offend them. Also, these organizations and groups are all prime sources for raising capital.

One way to draw interest in a show is to tap into the current headlines. I recently helped support a revival of Larry Kramer's *The Normal Heart*, a show from twenty years ago that approaches the topic of gay marriage, which is once again very much in the newspapers and a hot political topic. Inspired by the McCarthy hearings in the late 1940s, Arthur Miller's *The Crucible*, which draws a parallel to the witch hunts in the American colonies, ten years later, resurfaced with strong results. When the nation is involved in a war, a university may be a good place for an antiwar production, such as one from David Rabe's trilogy from the late 1960s. Rabe wrote about his own experiences in Vietnam, where he served in a hospital support unit, and went on to write *The Basic Training of Pavlo Hummel*, *Sticks and Bones*, and *Streamers*. Arthur Miller's play *All My Sons*, about ammunitions manufacturers, might also be relevant during wartime. Since many topical, political, and cultural issues resurface with each new generation, it is worthwhile to check out some older shows that spoke to a previous generation and see if they are relevant to your demographic group. Keep in mind, however, that you also want to entertain. If you can strike a good balance between presenting an issue and entertaining your audience, you may have found yourself a winner.

Caution: Politics and Religion

There are so many marvelous plays to choose from that it is easy to steer clear of shows based on the "hot buttons" of politics and religion. Political satires are tricky unless you are performing for a group that is obviously leaning in one direction, such as the Young Democrats or Young Republicans. Christmas shows notwithstanding, if you are looking for a fundraiser that won't stir up too many patrons, avoid anything that deviates from the norm when it comes to religion. The Manhattan Theater Club, in 1998, put on a production by established, award-winning playwright Terrance McNally called *Corpus Christi*. The play considered the question, what if Jesus was gay? Not only did subscribers to the theatre cancel their subscriptions, but the theatre received bomb threats, and groups of protestors marched in the streets. Initially, the club decided to cancel the production; however, after a statement in support of the theatre's right to put on the production was signed by Actors' Equity, the American Society of Journalists and Authors, the New York Foundation for the Arts, and the New York Screen Actors Guild, as well as many notable individuals including Arthur Miller and Stephen Sondheim, the theatre decided to go forward and stage *Corpus Christi*. Despite continuing threats of violence and the need for increased security in the venue, the show went on without incident.

An article on the website talkinbroadway.com summed up the *Corpus Christi* situation with a subtitle that read: "Why Producers Get Ulcers." The point being, don't subject your players to such situations unless they too are ready and willing to handle the potential backlash of a controversial show. Consider the potential ramifications of any play you choose, particularly if you are responsible to a larger group, such as your school.

Political correctness is part of our culture today. You need to be aware of the possible objections that may be raised by a community regarding your selection of a show. At the same time, remember the value and significance of freedom of speech. Weigh both sides of the issue carefully.

A Musical or a "Straight" Play?

The great debate: Should there be singing and dancing or should we do something dramatic, or even comedic? I almost always go with the musical, but several factors will influence your decision. Do you have anyone with musical talent? It certainly helps. While musicals are usually crowd pleasers, they typically require more space and more rehearsal time. In many cases they also have larger casts, which allows you to include more performers. A musical can be a lot of fun to put on and a great way to bring a large group together, whether they are performing or working backstage.

Dramatic plays present a more powerful message. Classic dramas such as *Death of a Salesman*, *The Glass Menagerie*, *Cat on a Hot Tin Roof*, and *A Streetcar Named Desire* are shows that have stood the test of time.

While evaluating your options, you need to consider the talent level and ability of your cast members; the age level and interests of your audience; and, of course, your reasons for putting on a show. Are you:

- Honing skills?
- Making a significant statement?
- Using a show as an educational tool?
- Raising money?

- Showcasing existing talent?
- All of the above?

Both musicals and straight plays can accomplish these goals.

It also helps to know who you have in your corner. Do you have a musical director at your disposal or someone who can serve in such a capacity? Do you have a choreographer or perhaps a volunteer versed in teaching dance? You will need someone with the ability to handle the musical portion of the show, as well as the dance sequences if such numbers are included.

When I was in high school, we did two shows a year, mostly plays because the theatre department wouldn't talk to the music department and vice versa. This is still one of the biggest problems today in many schools and universities that have theatre programs. Each one wants to control the show. Your decision may be made for you based on which department is putting on the production or in which department your allegiance lies.

If you are working with some experienced performers, elect to utilize their strengths. Do you have several particularly strong vocalists? Are some of your performers from a trained dance background? If you know that several of your performers are very well versed in a particular style of dance (modern or tap, for instance), look for a show that will allow them to demonstrate their talents. Go with your strengths when selecting a show.

Looking for Something Educational?

As well as raising money, entertaining the community, and honing the skills of the performers, shows performed in schools should have an educational foundation. I recall a show we put on in high school in the 1960s called *In White America*, by Martin Duberman. The show consisted of a series of letters and quotes from both black and white Americans on what it was like living in the United States. The authors ranged from a doctor aboard an eighteenth-century slave ship to a young black girl attempting to enter an all-white high school in 1957. The show involved a lot of the black and white students and brought home the serious issue of race relations. It was the first time I saw this topic approached in the theatre and it was a powerful learning and personal experience. Shows such as *The Crucible* or Sherman Edwards and Peter Stone's musical *1776*, about the Continental Congress and the signing of the Declaration of Independence, are clearly works with historical messages. Other educational options might include James Goldman's *The Lion in Winter*, Robert Oxton Bolt's *A Man for All Seasons*, or *Doubt*, John Patrick Shanley's recent production in which a nun's concerns about the possible improprieties of a priest touches on recent newspaper headlines. Remember, you can educate all ages, not only young children.

Of course, plenty of shows will spark educational discussions, including the works of Shakespeare. One high school did excerpts from *The Taming of the Shrew*, in which they had to edit out the line "My tongue in your tail." It all boils down to the age of the audience, the appropriate level of education, and students' maturity when it comes to handling the subject matter, and, in some cases, the likelihood of enraging the local school board. Schools frequently wrestle with the appropriate time to introduce certain works of Shakespeare.

Many plays for children are available from children's theatre publishing companies found throughout the country. The shows include many originals and short adaptations of popular fairy tales. From *Little Red Riding Hood* to the comedic *MacBeth—The Musical Comedy*, these short plays are designed to introduce children to the art of theatre while providing both education and fun. Pioneer Drama Service, home to seven hundred plays, allows you to search for plays on their website (www.pioneerdrama.com) based on cast size, running time, and type of play. Bad Wolf Press, another children's theatre publishing house, offers what they call "musical plays for musically timid teachers" (www.badwolfpress.com). The shows, running from fifteen to fifty minutes, are designed for grades K–9 and provide lessons through song and clever, age-appropriate dialogue.

The drama department at Northwestern University also provides a listing of children's play publishing houses at http://facultyweb.at.northwestern.edu/theater/tya/publishers.html.

Timeless, Timely, or Past Its Time?

Some shows will almost always work. They have a timeless story and a message that transcends the generations. Among the reasons I decided to bring *Fiddler on the Roof* back to Broadway in 2004 is that it is one of the five greatest musicals ever, and had not been on

Broadway in twenty years, which I thought was a crime. With three daughters who had never seen the show on Broadway, I thought about the fact that an entire generation had not seen *Fiddler* on the Great White Way. Something had to be done, so I brought it back, and sure enough, *Fiddler* was a hit with another generation of theatregoers. Ironically, *Fiddler* is a hit not only in America, but plays very successfully in Japan, where tradition and family are messages that transcend the language and cultural difference.

Other timeless musicals include Lerner and Loewe's *My Fair Lady* and Rodgers and Hammerstein's *Sound of Music* as well as *Oklahoma!* and, of course, *Guys and Dolls*. One of my personal favorites, by Arthur Laurents, with the music of Jule Styne and lyrics of Stephen Sondheim, is *Gypsy*. It may not be the right choice for some schools or religious groups, but it is a classic musical. A show such as Jim Jacobs and Warren Casey's 1950s rocker *Grease* is also a perennial favorite, as is *The Wizard of Oz* or even the updated version from William Brown and Charlie Smalls, *The Wiz*. One school production utilized twenty minutes from *The Wizard of Oz*, *The Wiz*, and *Wicked* in a one-hour presentation paying tribute to the ongoing legacy of the original classic. The Elvis-inspired *Bye Bye Birdie* from Michael Stewart, Charles Strouse, and Lee Adams, and *The Little Shop of Horrors* are fun musicals that have benefited from a new generation, many of whom have seen them on video. Both will usually work as crowd pleasers. *Annie* is a staple of the younger school set, and *Peter Pan* is another example of a show that never gets tired. The book holds up very well today. In the nonmusical genre, many of the Neil Simon comedies work well, such as *The Odd Couple* or *Sweet Charity*. For an older crowd, *The Sunshine Boys* also shines. George S. Kaufman and Moss Hart's *The Man Who Came to Dinner* and *You Can't Take It with You* and Shakespeare's *As You Like It*, are among the "can't miss" comedies.

Conversely, there are musicals in which the book does not hold up as well today, such as *Can Can*, by Abe Burrows (who also did the book for *Guys and Dolls*), despite a great Cole Porter score. The book for *Cabaret*, by Joe Masteroff, also had a dated feel to it until it was revised on its return to Broadway, with new musical numbers added. *On the Town* by Broadway legends Betty Comden and Adolph Green is another example of a show that may seem dated. Many shows are past their prime and may not inspire your players or speak to your audience. Even a play such as Michael Butler's *Hair*, a huge hit in the 1960s, is such a time-specific counterculture piece that, unless you are specifically presenting "a return to the sixties" festival or tribute, the audience today might not relate to it.

It's important to sit down and read through the book before making a decision on a show. Does the dialogue seem dated or does it speak to your audience? Are there issues that your demographic group can relate to? Is there a tie-in to something going on in the world today? In some instances, the story itself is timeless. In other instances, the director's interpretation can breathe new life into a show. Often, we see revivals of shows and then comment on what it was that made the particular version unique.

The right musical, even from a bygone era, can stand the test of time. Not only does the story still work, but the music is strong. For example, I agreed to produce the 1967 Richard Morris film *Thoroughly Modern Millie* into a Broadway show some thirty-five years after the movie was released. The story was set in the 1920s but it was not based on the cultural trends or politics of the era. It was very theatrical and there was a musical base to it. That's why *Millie* translated very well into a musical with an entertaining story for the stage. We took a cinematic movie and created a different animal, making it an original theatrical event, relying more on theatre tricks than cinematic tricks.

Sometimes, the basic good guy–bad guy element is the bridge between then and now, as was the case with Billy Wilder's 1959 film *Some Like It Hot*, set in the gangster era of the 1920s. Two musicians dressing as women to escape gangsters looking to rub them out has immediate comedic overtones—plus Marilyn Monroe didn't hurt. The stage version came to Broadway in 1972 and was called *Sugar* after Marilyn Monroe's character in the film. Once again, the story carried the show from the 1920s to the 1970s. Unfortunately, the musical didn't draw very favorable reviews and the show flopped. But as long as the book does not seem old or out of touch with today's audience, a musical based on the 1920s, '30s or '40s can work very well.

A Group Decision

Whether you are the teacher, dean of the drama department, or head of a fundraising committee, if you are in the position of deciding which show to put on, you may want to include your players in the process. But first, however, take some time to make a list of all of the factors discussed and then fill in the blanks. You might list:

- number or performers or anticipated number of performers
- budget
- resources (props, costumes, etc.) available
- someone who could serve as a musical director
- size of stage area (you may simply put small, medium, or large, based on how many people and how much scenery you realistically think will fit—*Hint:* Be conservative in your estimate)
- reason(s) for putting on the productions (i.e., to raise money and educate students)
- sufficient rehearsal space
- a set time frame until the show (Do you have only three weeks, or do you have as long as you like?)

All of this, in addition to your personal schedule, will need to be factored into the equation. Keep in mind that if you end up producing a large show, your personal life may be put on hold for several weeks, or even months.

Once you have made your list, in conjunction with the list here, select three or four possibilities and present them to everyone who will be involved in the production. Get input from the group. They may have creative ideas about how to make one show work over the other selections. In addition, you may find that several of your cast and crew members are more familiar with a particular show, or feel that a certain script would best represent the group or class. By allowing everyone to get involved in the selection process, you are providing ownership in the production, and where there is ownership there is usually greater enthusiasm. (*Hint:* Clear all your choices with the powers that be in advance—whether that means the dean, principal, board of directors, or whoever can possibly put the kibosh on your plans.) It can be worthwhile to share all your reasons for selecting the specific shows that you are presenting as possibilities. You may have overlooked something that might make one of your choices either the most or least likely candidate for your purposes.

If you are making the selection with other people, make it clear that once a decision is made, you expect that everyone will get on board, even if it was not their first choice. No matter what show is selected, there will be some compromises along the way, and everyone involved will need to exercise some flexibility for the good of the show.

And in the End

Once you have made the decision, alone or with the help of your cast and crew, you need to get behind your choice 100 percent and not second guess yourself. The more factors you have taken into account, the more likely it is that you have chosen the right show for your performers and for your demographic audience.

Getting Organized

Putting the Pieces Together

We started out doing the musical *Thoroughly Modern Millie* in La Jolla, California, under a regional theatre contract, which meant we could not afford to get an actual elevator in the show. In the movie, the elevator was almost another character. In fact, there's a whole dance number in the elevator, and they utilize it throughout the movie. On stage, however, you can stylize things, using light and sounds to create the effects you need, and it worked out very well in La Jolla. But when we came to Broadway, the authors insisted on having a real elevator onstage. "It's major, it's important to the show," they kept telling me.

I explained that an elevator is not an inexpensive thing to purchase—this is a big-ticket item at about $300,000. It didn't matter. They kept saying, "You've got to have the elevator." So, I acquiesced, and sure enough, we had an elevator onstage during the previews.

As we worked on the show during the previews I noticed that the elevator had become more of a hindrance than an asset. It took people too long to go up and down, and watching people riding in an elevator was akin to watching paint dry. The audience sits there waiting for something to happen.

As the previews continued, we began cutting out the elevator—a little here, a little there—and by the time we were finished, we used the elevator only twice in the show. Once was to stage an existing number and the second time was a token moment because we had a $300,000 elevator sitting there. It was one of those expenses that we could easily have avoided but sometimes to please your talent, you simply *gotta do what you gotta do.* Ultimately everyone involved learned a valuable lesson.

Possibly the most important skill when producing a show is keeping your wits about you when everyone else has lost theirs. You may recall Dr. Seuss' *Cat in the Hat* character, balancing a fish bowl on an umbrella in one hand, a bottle of milk on a book in the other, and a cake and a tea pot on his head while standing atop a ball. Quite a feat you may think. In fact, it's child's play next to producing a show. It is to your advantage before auditions, casting, rehearsals, selling tickets, or taking a bow to take a step back and go through the various elements of your upcoming production.

This chapter takes a brief look at several pieces of the production jigsaw puzzle. With any luck, you will find skilled individuals to head up your creative team and provide knowledge in the specific areas listed later. If not, you will simply have to wing it, taking into consideration some of the tips and recommendations offered in the individual sections.

Since theatre existed long before film, television, or the Internet, it's safe to say that much of what can be done by using computer software and the latest in technology can also be done by using a mixture of creativity, ingenuity, and good old-fashioned common sense. Safety concerns aside, there are very few definitive "rights" and "wrongs" when working in the theatre. Producers and directors often stray from what might be considered the "traditional approach" while following their vision. Instead of *Julius Caesar* being done in ancient Rome, Orson Welles placed it in mid-twentieth century America. It is this nonconformist approach that makes theatre such a distinctive form of artistic expression.

In this chapter we touch on ten important areas that producers need to take into account. There are many possible approaches to these aspects of production, but all should be considered early on in the process. Some topics discussed are elaborated on in subsequent chapters, while others simply provide food for thought.

1. The budget
2. Ground rules
3. Rehearsal space
4. Wardrobe — *Mgr,*
5. Scenery *Carpenta ?*
6. Properties (props) *PROP Masta PROP LIST*
7. Set and prop changes *Stage Mgr.*
8. Stage lighting *Lighty Direch*
9. Sound system
10. Publicity

Clearly, other issues will need to be addressed; however, these are the most common ones that producers focus on during preproduction. Once you have examined each aspect of the production in advance, it will be easier to respond to questions, delegate responsibilities, establish a time line and keep tabs on the progress of your creative team without losing your mind.

The Budget — *Track Eypenses Page*

This is theatre, so in some cases your budget is whatever you find between the cushions of the couch in the teacher's lounge. While many producers find themselves working with little or no money, some schools, community theatre groups, or children's theatres are able to stay afloat thanks to the generosity of benefactors, previous ticket sales, or a sizable endowment. Repertory theatres may or may not have much funding, depending on how long they have been in existence and how well they have drawn audiences in previous seasons. Whatever your situation, utilize what you have carefully, especially since everyone involved with the show will have suggestions as to how you should spend your available funds.

Regardless of the size and scope of the production and budget, find someone trustworthy to help you by handling the money and bookkeeping, This will allow you to focus on other aspects of production while still knowing exactly how much funding you have available. This individual should be well-organized, keep good records, and have the uncanny ability to say "no" to the numerous requests for money. A general manager can be appointed to oversee the budget, or you can have a treasurer maintain financial records and write out checks. As producer, you should have the final authorization on all spending as it relates to the production.

Here is a sample budget for a play, based on one used by a university theatre department in Texas:

Expected support from the School of Theatre = $700

Budget

Rights	$50 (to Samuel French for rights to the show)
Scripts	$100 (copies)
Scenery	$100 (lumber for walls and paint)
Costumes	$100 (cleaning and purchase of items not in stock)
Properties	$100 (purchase of props not in stock)
Lighting	$75 (gels and templates not in stock)
Publicity	$100 (flyers, programs, posters)
Miscellaneous	$75 (which should include a tip for the custodian who helped you clean up or for anyone else who helped you out)
TOTAL	$700

It is typically more costly to put on a musical than a play, with the need for more rehearsals, musicians, and all that goes into staging a musical. On Broadway, a play can be staged for approximately $2 million, while a musical will typically $10 to $15 million (depending on the size of the cast).

The key to maintaining a budget is to have the money filter through one person—the general manager, the treasurer or you—and to document all expenditures. No one, including the producer, should be exempt from following procedure when it comes to documenting expenses.

Before our sample budget was put together, an inventory was taken to determine what the department had on hand and what they would have to purchase. Determine how much funding to appropriate for each area—wardrobe, props, sets, advertising, and so on. Of course, be flexible and prepared to reallocate funds as necessary, particularly if you can barter rather than spend to cover some of your needs. For example, if you provide a local radio station with tickets in exchange for air time to promote your show, then you are saving money that you can move to another part of your budget.

In some cases, items you had budgeted for purchase may be donated. This, too, will allow you to reallocate funding. If you need three tuxedos and there is just one in your theatre department wardrobe, you may allocate money toward renting the other two. Should someone in your cast suddenly discover that his or her grandfather has three tuxedos in his attic and is willing to let you have them for the show, the money can then be moved from tuxedo rental to another area, such as publicity. You can give a "thanks to" acknowledgment in the program for the donation. You might also find that the neighborhood tuxedo rental shop is happy to lend you three tuxedos in exchange for a mention in your program. Never underestimate the power of being associated with a noble production. And remember, giving credit to local merchants goes a long way.

This principle holds true for theatre companies at all levels. The budget may be larger and spread out across an entire season, but flexibility, the use of barter, and the need for one dedicated person to handle the funds is always the same.

Ground Rules

In baseball, the umpires meet at home plate prior to each game to discuss the specific ground rules for each stadium so that everyone knows what is considered fair, what is foul, and what is a home run. In the theatre, have similar discussions before signing a contract with the theatre manager or owner. Just like the umpires, the board of directors, principal of the school, landlord of a rented space, or anyone in charge of the venue in which you will be holding your show will have their own rules and regulations, which will need to be explained.

No smoking is common in many public places, but, other rules may apply that you are not aware of. For instance, you may or may not be able to serve food, soft drinks, or alcohol, depending on where you are holding the performance. There may be certain displays in a school that are not to be taken down and certainly in a house of worship you do not want to be sacrilegious by draping your scenery over sacred religious artifacts.

Besides the rules imposed by venues, you will find trade unions with contracts stating that only their workers can handle certain jobs or local zoning regulations that may also impact your plans. For instance, you may not be allowed to deliver twelve pounds of hay through the front entrance to feed the horse in Peter Shaffer's *Equus* or you may not be allowed to do a production of The Who's rock opera *Tommy* at decibel levels that could drown out the local airport.

From where you can put signage to who will clean up after the show, whoever is responsible for the theatre, hall, auditorium, or garage will want to make sure you know the rules. Fire laws always need to be adhered to. There are strict rules that may include fire-proofing and using fire retardants on almost everything in the theatre. Make sure that exits from the auditorium are clear for passage and that all stairwells are well lit. While these are generally the responsibilites of the theatre owner, you cannot impinge upon the safety precautions or procedures that have been established. You want to make sure you provide a safe, secure environment for yourself and your cast and crew. In fact, theatre companies may want to have insurance as protection should someone in the cast, crew, or audience be injured during a rehearsal or production.

While using a theatre space, your goal is to have as little impact on the facility as possible—in other words, when you leave, the venue should be exactly as you found it. That will help ensure that should you choose to utilize the same space in the future, you will be able to do so. Even in schools, the drama or theatre department is responsible to the school or university for adhering to the rules of the playhouse, concert hall, auditorium, or wherever the show is being presented. More on this is discussed in the next chapter on choosing a venue.

Rehearsal Space — TBA, ms besemant? my lounge?

We touched on the topic earlier, but warrants repeating: secure your rehearsal space early on. This will allow you to plan a schedule, so that once you have your cast and creative team in place, they can start rehearsals.

If the stage is either not available on a regular basis or too costly, both of which are often the case, you will need to find another, comparable space. Remember, since the budget is typically a concern, think barter rather than rent. I recall doing a showcase in Los Angeles of an early version of my play *In the Wings*. I had joined a local synagogue, and when it came time to find rehearsal space, I asked the director of the synagogue if I could use their classrooms at night. They were fine with the idea, since the rooms were not being used, and we promised to leave them in the same shape as we found them. We thanked them with a byline in the program, and free preview tickets for the congregation. Years later, when rehearsing *The Will Rogers Follies* for Broadway with *Tommy Tune* we were able to use the Nederlander, another Broadway theatre that was dark at that time. *Tommy Tune* had earlier rehearsed the original version of the show *Nine* in a small, little-known theatre space atop what was then the defunct New Amsterdam, which, after renovations, went on to be home to Disney's *The Lion King* and *Mary Poppins*. The small theatre space high atop the large venue was used years earlier by Flo Ziegfield for his private shows. It remains unused today.

In a small community you need to be equally creative. For example, you may have a number of nine-to-fivers, who are only available in the evening. Look for space in schools during the evenings, at community centers, or even in a warehouse, like the one used by the dance team in the film version of *The Full Monty*. Some libraries have rooms that go unused after five or six o'clock. Occasionally apartment buildings or condos have a common area or clubhouse that is available. The key is to look around, leave no stone unturned, and be ready to barter before spending cash.

Once you find a rehearsal space, make sure to look it over carefully. As with negotiating your theatre space, discuss the ground rules. Producers and directors are sometimes anxious to find a rehearsal space, and the other party is more than happy to be a part of the theatre experience (and doesn't mind the free mention in the program, either). Unfortunately, in their haste, the producers/directors fail to notice aspects of the facility that may be hazardous, since this space is not normally used for a chorus line of dancers. Always think safety first—for your cast, your crew, and, once inside your theatre space, for your customers.

In your rehearsal space, make sure wiring is out of the way; computers and other equipment can be safely moved if necessary and other potential disasters dealt with ahead of time. I can't tell you how many accidents happen when people try to take shortcuts and don't follow the rules. If an accident does occur, be forthright with whoever provided the space. Your goal should be to get in, do a smooth rehearsal, and get out, leaving the facility as you found it.

Wardrobe

Wardrobe is an integral part of any production and can enhance a show if approached carefully with an eye for authenticity and style. British theatre designer Peter Ruthren Hall said, "Before a character even speaks, we 'read' their appearance through their costume." To give you a head start, most scripts purchased from a companies like Samuel French, Dramatic Play Service, or other licensing houses, will include a list of what each character will wear in the show. For example, it might say:

> matching light brown vest and cuffed pants
>
> dark brown tweed jacket
>
> white shirt
>
> green tie
>
> brown wing-tip shoes

It will be up to whomever you name as your wardrobe supervisor to find, make, buy, beg, borrow, or (hopefully not) steal each item on the list.

In a repertory theatre company or a school with a large, active theatre department, it is likely that you will have at least a few of your costume needs readily at hand—with some necessary alterations, of course. Keep in mind that you can also borrow from other schools and institutions. There might be a theatre company in the next county that would lend you some of their costumes for a "thank-you" credit in your program. If the company or theatre department has put on a production of the same show in recent years, you may be in luck and they might still have costumes.

In elementary through high school productions, a volunteer with a creative flair and a sewing machine will often become your closest ally when it comes to meeting your wardrobe needs. It is to your advantage, especially when dealing with a large cast of children, to get started on this aspect of the show early on, allowing plenty of time for cast members to try on costumes and complete all necessary alterations.

Consider ways to make costume changes as simple as possible, especially for younger children, and, for everyone, how practical the costume will be on stage. If the costume prohibits movement, is too heavy, or makes it virtually impossible to hear the character's dialogue, you will need to rethink the character's wardrobe. Costumes should look authentic but also allow for ease of movement.

Costumes worn onstage include not only the actual clothing, but the hair, make-up, and accessories that, combined, will create the overall look, manner, and personalities of the characters. Texture, pattern, and color each convey a number of different messages, including the socioeconomic class of the character, cultural norms, the time of year, or the period in history.

Work within your budget and use all available resources to get as close as possible to the look you want to create. After all, if a dark-blue coat is listed and you can only come up with a gray one, no one is likely to make a fuss, *unless the play is about the Civil War.*

Children's theatre also presents a common, and somewhat intriguing, costuming challenge. Many shows written for young audiences have their fair share of ghosts, ghouls, goblins, monsters, and talking animals. You may need to work with your wardrobe supervisor to create costumes that will not frighten a young audience. For this reason, among others, the highly creative animal costumes in Disney's *The Lion King* were designed so that you could see the actual person and not just the animal costume. It also permitted greater movement for the performers, who had to dance as animals.

Scenery

Scenic artists and set designers have been honing their craft for centuries. From the brilliantly handcrafted work of the Renaissance era to the hi-tech tools used by scenic artists today, scenic design has always combined artistic talent with technical skills. Mechanical drawing, image reproduction, and drafting are the necessary technical skills, while painting, drawing, calligraphy, and sign painting are among the creative aspects of scenic design. The goal of fusing these technical and artistic skills is to create a visual world within which the story will unfold.

For all these students, myself included, who recall thinking in high school that there would never be a practical use for geometry, well here it is. Prior to creating a set design for the stage, someone has to draw it on paper. That drawing must be to scale with what you will use onstage, and that necessitates the use of geometry. After all, when you draw something that will later be built, you want to be certain it will fit the stage and be the proper height and width for your needs. Rob Reiner's comedic 1984 film *Spinal Tap* illustrates the point well. Members of a fictitious rock band ask the stage designer to build a model of the historic rock formation Stonehenge. The set designer receives the instructions to build each of the rock forms twelve inches high. When the band walks onto the stage, they trip over the tiny rock formations which were supposed to be twelve feet high. In *March of the Wooden Soldiers*, the film version of *Babes in Toyland* with Laurel and Hardy, Santa puts an order in for six-hundred soldiers one foot high, but Laurel and Hardy accidentally put in an order for one hundred soldiers six feet high. They end up saving Toy Land, but you see, your measurements need to be precise.

Drafting involves drawing the object you want to represent to scale. This means that a certain increment represents one foot. Most work for theatre is drawn at 1/2 inch = 1 foot or 1/4 inch = 1 foot. No matter how precise your drawings are, have a good idea of how your set designs will translate to the stage. You want the scenery to be easily visible from the audience's perspective as well as suitable for the play. You don't want Juliet on a balcony that is only a half foot off the ground, or the Fiddler on the roof blocked by the orchestra.

Some plays will come with photos or diagrams of the staging and the sets. These are usually from a director or set designer. While this will help limit the geometry portion of the job, you still need to do some measuring to make sure you know exactly how much space you have onstage and what you can build to fit the space.

Whether constructing a set from plywood or using a large canvas, work with your most artistic volunteers to measure and plan carefully before painting. Young (and older) students are often very eager to start painting the background, but if your show takes place in Paris and they run out of room before painting an Eiffel Tower, Paris will not come to the minds of your audience. Plan carefully before you, or anyone else, starts painting.

Like wardrobe, scenery can say a lot to the audience about the setting, the time of year, the climate, the time period in which the play occurs, and even the socioeconomic conditions at the time the play takes place. Scenery also needs to work in conjunction with your props, particularly large ones, such as furniture. For this reason, many designers build from the furnishings outward.

Prior to all of this, it is worthwhile to go out and do some research on the time period and location of the show. If you are working with an original play, you will have to work from your own research since you will not have prior set diagrams to use for reference. The Internet is a great place to find period photos and drawings to illustrate anything, from a turn-of-the-century farmhouse to a futuristic space station. Photos and illustrations can bring your vision of the scenery into a realistic backdrop that meets the needs of your show. For a basic box set (representing the interior of a room) look closely at photographs of a living room or dining room from the time period. Look at details and see if you can reproduce them in some manner.

Once you have the set you want on paper, allocate funds in your budget for buying materials to commence set building. This is also when you will need to make a detailed shopping list of supplies—some of which (like hammers and screwdrivers) can be borrowed from cast and crew members—or may be available in the school, community center, or wherever you are staging the show. Keep in mind that if schools have shop or woodworking courses, scenery can become a class project. Otherwise, you will probably be seeking volunteers to do some set building.

This is also a time when safety becomes a significant concern, especially if children or teens are involved. If kids are helping build the set, they must work with adult supervision at all times or else you are inviting potential disaster. Use all commonsense safety measures, which include putting all tools away safely, wearing goggles, dust masks, gloves, and so on. Make sure that each and every item built is sturdy and properly supported, and will not come crashing down during rehearsals or a performance.

Other safety concerns include:

- Providing proper ventilation while painting or using any cleaning materials
- Compliance with all fire and building safety laws
- Moving planks of wood and any other large items in and out of your space safely. (Are there special freight entrances you should be using?)
- Checking out all movable parts of your set to make sure they work and are safe (i.e., doors and windows need to open and close without causing anyone injury)
- Keeping all necessary supplies in a safe place (i.e., wood, nails, hammers, saws, other building tools, paper and writing utensils, paint, paintbrushes, rollers, drop clothes, etc.)
- Determining whether students (or adults) have allergies or are asthma suffers
- Safe cleanup and storage after each day of set building and painting; nothing "lying around"
- Easy and safe transporting of scenery during show and after
- If you are planning on doing several productions, or have the budget and requirements for a more elaborate set, look for a copy of *Backstage Handbook: An Illustrated Almanac of Technical Information*, by Paul Carter and George Chiang, which describes in great detail all backstage operations, including building and painting scenery.

Having said all of this, there is always the option of doing a show such as Thornton Wilder's *Our Town*, where you won't need to build a set at all. Other shows work very well with minimalist set designs, including all Shakespeare's works, the Tom Jones–Harvey Schmidt musical *The Fantasticks*, Samuel Beckett's *Waiting for Godot*, Edward Albee's *The Zoo Story*, or Howard Sackler's *The Great White Hope*, where all you need is a wagon to come on and tell you here we are in Germany or here we are in France. There were also plays in the 1950s and '60s that were specifically designed to step away from the more traditional theatre productions and worked well with minimalist settings.

Properties (Props)   PROP LIST

Properties, or props, as they are better known, are all those items
that fill up the stage and are used by your actors throughout the
show. From simple props such as a deck of cards for the poker game
in *The Odd Couple* to a giant man-eating plant in *The Little Shop of
Horrors*, props add the necessary details to the story. A prop list will
usually accompany a published show. For a new show, one needs
to be made up based on the script. Either way, once you have a prop
list, the scavenger hunt begins. Your budget for props should include only the hard-to-find items that are essential for the show.
Top hats from the early 1900s, for example, may be necessary to
illustrate the time period and may need to be rented.

A theatre company or drama department of a university will
likely have a greater inventory to rummage through than will a community theatre group, grade school, or middle school. Props are
frequently borrowed and not returned, so don't be disappointed if
there are not a lot of items readily available. Ingenuity, creativity,
and the old fallback—borrowing from friends, neighbors, and relatives, are ways in which you can start to whittle away at the prop
list. The following is a partial prop list from Bob Hall and David
Richmond's Off-Broadway show, *The Passion of Dracula*.

    feather duster
    coffee tray with cups saucers and silver pots
    metal crash tray
    Jameson's gun
    two lanterns
    straightjacket
    tray with sandwiches
    four garlic strands
    swooping bat
    Helga's bloody blouse
    wind machine
    fog machine
    bloody handkerchief
    book

transfusion equipment

bandages

Clearly, a book or bandages will be easier to find than a wind machine. Of course, a well-positioned offstage fan might serve your purpose. Sometimes you simply need to create what you do not have, while in other cases, you need the authentic appearance of the object. Starter guns, for example, are typically easier to be had than fake prop guns. *Hint:* It is important today to make sure that all appropriate security personnel, especially in a school, know that a fake gun or starter pistol is on the premises and being used for the play. Incidents of props, such as guns, swords, and fake knives being confiscated have become more common with today's need for tighter security in schools.

Whomever you put in charge of props should begin the hunt early on. This way you will know if the $100 or $200 you budgeted for props is more or less than adequate. Among the prop sources on the Internet, you will find places like Theatre House, based in Covington, Kentucky, which has an extensive website listing thousands of props by categories from Roman armor to Mary Antoinette wigs. You can find them at www.theatrehouse.com or by calling (800) 827-2414. In recent years, eBay has also become the place to meet your offbeat props needs. Set designer Paul Wosnek, of the Walnut Street Theatre in Philadelphia, picked up a 1930s Sears & Roebuck catalog on eBay in search of furnishings for Neil Simon's *Lost in Yonkers*. Although the play was set in the '40s, Wosnek assumed that Grandma Krunitz would have purchased her furniture years earlier, which was why he opted for the 1930s catalog. Your goal should be to get as close to the prop list as possible, while staying within your budget.

Set and Prop Changes

Set and prop changes are the job of the stage manager, but unless you are producing shows for a theatre company or happen to have an experienced stage manager ready and willing to volunteer, much of this responsibility (like many others) will fall on your shoulders. Have a realistic plan in place for scene changes. Will the curtain close or lights dim between scenes? Will you use a process called *a vista*, which is common in many productions and refers to changing the scenery in full view of the audience? This is usually accomplished by the stage crew dressed in black and working in 20 percent light. This process needs to be rehearsed several times so that crew members know exactly what is to be moved and where it is headed. If you do not have much room in the wings or have limited crew members, you will have to find ways to utilize your set while changing objects or drape a painted back cloth over the scenery for a different look.

Of course, many shows take place in one setting and make your life infinitely easier, such as Neil Simon's *The Odd Couple*, which takes place entirely in Oscar Madison's living room; Jerome Lawrence and Robert E. Lee's *Inherit the Wind*, which takes place solely in the court room; the Reginald Rose drama *Twelve Angry Men*, which took place in the jury room; or Bernard Slade's *Same Time, Next Year*, which is in one hotel room—only the décor changes to show the passage of time. Many other shows fall into this category, from classic old shows like *Life with Father* by Russel Crouse to recent shows such as *Tales of the Allergist's Wife*, a comedy by Charles Busch.

When I wrote *In the Wings*, the only set used was that of the young actor's home. When it became a musical, the songs were performed in front of a curtain that dropped. To indicate another location, characters can speak in front of the curtain or off to the side of the set (in a spotlight) or hold a simple prop, like a steering wheel, to indicate they are riding in a car.

Make sure everyone knows where all necessary props should be prior to, and during, the show. Prop tables should be located on stage left and stage right, and everything that is used should be returned to the tables when you are done. Before every production, always make sure the props are on the tables, since props often tend to move around on their own.

Ultimately, you want all scene transitions to be as smooth as possible, with both cast and crew members knowing what they are responsible for and where everything belongs.

Stage Lighting

From coffee cans with lightbulbs inside to the latest in hi-tech computerized lighting, schools, universities, and local theatres run the gamut with lighting equipment. Part of your job will be to assess what you have to work with and then determine who is comfortable—and, ideally experienced—at handling your lighting needs.

Theatrical lighting can be much more than just illuminating the stage. Using form, color, direction, and movement, a lighting director can set the tone and mood for a scene as well as signal the time of day or create one of many outdoor settings. By utilizing the available lighting tools, you can create a very real or hauntingly surreal atmosphere on stage. Lighting is also often used to direct the attention of the audience to a particular player or to signal a scene transition. It can even factor into the story line. In Frederick Knott's *Wait Until Dark*, for example, the absence of light is crucial to the final scene.

While electric lighting debuted in the twentieth century, the use of lighting has long been part of theatre. In the outdoor theatres of ancient Greece, plays would be presented at certain times of day specifically to take advantage of the various types of natural lighting. Through the ages, torches, candles, and gas lights were also used as stage lights, although it was far more difficult to put colored gels on a torch.

The modern professional lighting director is constantly learning new and inventive ways to enhance the performance with stage lighting. He or she works hard to overcome complications that arise from props, costumes, and unwanted shadows, to name just a few of the many lighting challenges. While state-of-the-art lighting means working on a computerized control panel, most lighting systems require manual labor and a lot of hit-or-miss attempts before getting everything to look just right. Of course, the lighting director—or you as the case may be—will need to work in conjunction with the director, the performers, and the script to make sure the lighting is where you want it, when you want it, and at the level you want it. The stage going dark three seconds too soon or too late can be disastrous.

If you have the opportunity to use color, you can experiment further. Filters or gels can present numerous color options and are not very expensive. Be careful, however, because doubling-up gels can limit illumination and cause a lamp to get too hot. Considering the number of colors available, you should not need to do so. In fact, to keep gels from getting too hot, poke a few tiny holes in them before putting them onto a light.

The backdrop or scenery will also factor into your lighting decisions. White or pale colors will reflect light and present a more illuminated stage and a dark background will soak up more light.

If you have lighting options, you may decide to broadly flood the stage with a soft light so that everything is equally illuminated. Conversely, you might choose to localize lighting so that it is on your actors. You can also use backlighting on a performer to help separate the main subject from the background. Backlighting can have dramatic effects, particularly during a scene in which there is movement, such as a dance. It also gives the illusion of greater depth. Experienced lighting directors know how to set the lighting composition to fit the scene by revealing objects and performers in a manner that enhances the story.

Rosco International, at www.rosco.com, is among the leading sources for stage lighting (as well as scenic paint, art brushes, and fog machines). If you are in the market for stage lighting, you can save money by looking for used lights from local television stations or other theatre companies that may be moving or upgrading their own lighting system.

In general terms, stage lights are referred to as floodlights (floods) or spotlights (spots). Floodlights typically do not have a lens and are used to illuminate a broader area (flooding the area) while spotlights have lenses and can be more easily controlled to illuminate a specific performer, area, or prop.

Many smaller venues use Parabolic Aluminized Reflector lamps or PAR lamps, as they are more commonly known, along with scoop lights. The PAR lamps resemble the headlights on a car. In the theatre, PARs are most often used as top lights over the stage. Scoops are large circular lights you often see hanging in theatres. There is minimal control, if any, over the wide lighting pattern of scoops, but they can be inexpensive and serve your purposes.

The latest in moving lights (a/k/a, intelligent fixtures) are commonly found in theatre, television, and all stage environments. Color patterns, zoom, focus, diversity of the amount of light, and shape of the beam can all be controlled by computer or by someone working the lighting board.

Consider five key areas when it comes to stage lighting:

1. *Wiring:* Make sure wiring is secured so that it will not come unplugged and no one will trip over it.

2. *Power:* Know exactly how much electrical current the circuits can handle. If, for example, a circuit is 20 amps, then it can handle about 2,400 watts. Therefore, your stage lights must not exceed that amount. It is in your best interest to work with what the venue has or to add lighting only with the assistance of someone who is familiar with the electrical wiring of the building.

3. *Safety:* Lamps must be handled carefully. Be ready to shut down any lamp that has gotten too warm—smoke is a definite tipoff. Make sure to shut off stage lighting when you are not rehearsing or the performance is over.

4. *Your audience:* Don't blind them! Point lights away from your audience—unless, of course, that is your intent.

5. *The lighting board:* Make sure whoever is working the lighting has studied the technical script and rehearsed the lighting cues.

Sound System

Some thirty or forty years ago, most schools could not afford microphones. Today, like lighting, sound systems range from state-of-the-art to the most basic microphone and amplifier. In small settings you are often better without microphones, as they can be more trouble than they are worth.

Wireless microphones are the latest in stage accessories. If you are using wireless mikes, you or your sound engineer will need to find places to hide them on your performers. Typically they are hidden in the hair, under collars or anywhere else where they can be taped or clipped on, leaving some space from the body (in case the performer sweats).

Another option is to place microphones strategically on or above the stage so they are out of view of the audience but pick up the performers' voices. Typically, two or three well-placed area microphones can pick up sound from the stage while remaining out of view of the audience. Often, splitting the stage into thirds with three such microphones will suffice. With children, whose fidgeting may be picked up on a wireless mike, area microphones may be your answer. They can be set up at the lip of the stage or mounted on walls or even in props or scenery. Area microphones can have wires, since they will remain in one place, or you can use wireless ones, which cost a little more. If the facility already has microphones, you may be in luck.

Of course no matter which microphones you use, the quality of sound will depend largely on the sound system and the acoustics of the room. In most cases, these are two factors over which you will have little, if any, control. If you are in a position to bring in your own sound system, you can set up the system as you choose. Otherwise, you will have to make do with what is available. If you can position the speakers, experiment with positioning that will provide enough output for the entire room without distorting the performers' voices or blowing away the people sitting too close. Test various volume levels before committing to one. Stand in various places to see how well the sound travels.

If you are also using sound effects, make sure whoever is handling such effects knows their cues and is ready, since they are part of the scripted show. Pretest sound effects to make sure they provide the sounds you are seeking and are recorded at the same sound level so they are not too loud or too soft.

Here are five sound aspects to consider:

1. *Feedback:* Typically, the placement of speakers in conjunction with your microphones is the leading cause of feedback. When mikes are too close together or when the speakers are behind the microphone, you get feedback. You can discover during rehearsals if feedback is an issue and move the speakers accordingly. Watch the volume levels, which can also cause feedback. If someone is speaking into a handheld microphone, make sure they learn how far away from their mouth to hold the microphone during rehearsals. It's very common for people to hold microphones too close to their mouths, causing feedback or muddling the sound.

2. *Volume:* It's not a disco, so don't overdo it. The goal is to fill the room, not destroy it.

3. *Wires:* Just like the wires for lighting, make sure sound wires are taped to the floor or the walls so they do not pose a hazard. If a performer needs to use a microphone with a wire on stage, make sure he or she knows its range—

young children have been known to pull microphones just a little farther than they will go.

4. *Interference:* Radio Frequency hits (RFs) are not uncommon with wireless mikes. These are sound waves picked up from radio or television stations or police radios. You must make sure all wireless mikes are tuned to an unused channel in your area.

5. *Too much noise:* If you have someone working a sound console to control microphones, they should work in conjunction with your script and turn down, or shut off, all mikes that are not being used. This will prevent unwanted noise.

Most electronics stores, or those selling musical instruments, will carry microphones. Places on the Internet such as Audiogear.com (www.audiogear.com) carry a variety of models including name brands like Sony and Samson—you can also go to www.sony.com or www.samsontech.com or other manufacturers' websites and look around.

Publicity

The subject of publicity comes up later in the book when we talk about marketing your show in Chapter 9. However, publicity is something that should stay in your sphere of focus from day one. You can get a general idea, based on your production costs, how much will be left in the budget for your publicity needs. The rest is merely a matter of spreading the news through word of mouth and well-placed signs and posters.

During my early years in school productions, we worked with whatever we had. We designed posters and hung them in local shop windows. We still do that on Broadway to generate grassroots support for the show. If you walk around the Broadway district today, you'll notice posters of Broadway and Off-Broadway shows in all the local restaurants and shops.

Years ago, little money was allotted in the budget for printing and advertising, and many posters were hand drawn. Today, the advent of desktop publishing allows you to create fliers and signs from your own home. Kinko's and similar stores make it quick and easy to handle much of your printing needs.

All, or most, of these areas will typically be part of the process from day one. You may be fortunate to have enough people on your creative team so that you need only oversee their efforts. However, in many instances, you will fill only a few of these positions with able-bodied volunteers, and guess who will handle the remaining tasks? For this reason, it is up to you to start writing your "to-do" lists and get organized before becoming overwhelmed. This may mean utilizing your BlackBerry, desktop, laptop, or electronic organizer, or simply buying a notebook and labeling pages, "props," "lighting," "scenery," and so on. No matter how you do it, start planning how you will handle the many aspects of a production as early as possible.

Okay, now start juggling.

Finding a Performance Space

In the early 1980s I discovered a cute musical in Chicago called *A Change in the Heir*, based on a Mark Twain short story. The show was doing well and I decided to produce it at the Edison Theater on 47th Street, in New York City, a long-standing and very reputable theatre in the Edison Hotel. We had a very talented cast of actors, some of whom have gone on to do quite well, including J. K. Simmons, who was on the HBO series *Oz*, and did *Guys and Dolls* on Broadway. The director was a man who had won many Joseph Jefferson Awards, the Chicago equivalent of a Tony Award. He was known regionally as a terrific director.

The critics all planned to come on the Tuesday night before we were scheduled to open. We had the *New York Times*, *The Daily News*, and all the other big guns in the house. The curtain went up, the laughter started and it was going well. And then, not ten minutes into the show, an ear-piercing alarm went off. It was awfully loud and extremely annoying. The audience sat there wondering, "Is this part of the show?" And the blaring alarm kept going.

48

I told the director to stop the show onstage, and I ran into the Edison Hotel, which is a block long, with the theatre on one end and a nightclub on the other. It turns out that for whatever reason, on this particular night the chief of the fire department decided to test the alarm system at the nightclub, without realizing that it was also connected to the theatre.

So I shouted, "I've got a million-dollar show up there! I've got the *New York Times* here! They're all here!! How do you shut this damn thing off!" The more I shouted at him, the more I could see him start to harden up. His arms folded and the look told me, this approach is not working.

Okay, I thought, I'll take a different approach. *The Naked Ape.* "Excuse me sir, I know you have your job to do but I've got a lot of money riding here, a lot of investors, is there something that you could do to make this stop?"

He said, "Oh, I'm sorry. It's on a cycle. It takes another five minutes for it to end." So I ran back upstairs and we started up again from where we were. A couple of lost gags, but otherwise not much harm done. Then, five minutes later, the alarm went off again. Total pandemonium broke loose. The critics walked out, everyone left.

The director was in the green room, crying. "My career is over. I'll never work in this town again," he sobbed.

I'm tried to calm him down, "Don't say that—this is one of many shows we'll do. You'll see."

But you know what? He was right—he never worked in this town again.

From a swimming pool at Yale University to a garage in downtown Manhattan, theatre does not always have to be in an actual theatre. In fact, the ceremony in one of the long-running Off-Broadway shows, *Tony & Tina's Wedding*, by Artificial Intelligence, has taken place in part at St. John's and, later, St. Luke's churches in Greenwich Village, with the reception in Vinnie Black's Coliseum at the Edison Hotel. And who would have thought that the once-famous dance club of the late 1970s disco era, Studio 54, would be home to Bertolt Brecht and Kurt Weill's musical *The Threepenny Opera*?

As we've seen by the many of the works of Shakespeare that have been performed in various locations, shows can be adapted to work in spaces other than the traditional theatre and performed in various ways to fit to a specific space. The latest revival of the dark Sondheim musical *Sweeney Todd*, for example, does not even need an orchestra. The actors double as the musicians onstage. There was also a production of the show dubbed *Teeny Todd*, because the cast was cut down to only the principals. The abridged version (which did have an orchestra) earned four Tony Award nominations. The John Kander, Fred Ebb, Bob Fosse musical *Chicago* was brought back as a revue, featuring the songs from the show in concert format, with the orchestra on stage. There was just one set and no real costumes except the black tie and tuxedos for the guys and the fishnet stockings for the girls, to emphasize the time period. Sometimes rethinking a production can result in a new, scaled-down version of a larger show. When I did a production of *Ragtime* in London, we got rid of the large set and did more of a concert version. We were nominated for an Olivier Award for doing that. If you are planning to cut a show, write to the licensing company and let them know your plans. Most often, they will clear the idea with the appropriate source. You can also ask about abridged versions, which exist for many shows.

We'll return to the subject of unique theatre spaces and adaptations of shows later in this chapter. First, let's take a look at theatre rental.

You may find classified ads in local newspapers for theatres that have space for rent. Larger cities, such as Los Angeles and New York, have specific papers for the theatre community, such as *Back Stage* (with East and West Coast versions), which posts auditions and includes theatre information.

You can also surf the Web for theatre rental ads in your area. Of course, being proactive and contacting locations where there may be an available stage is also a great way to find a theatre. Look at colleges, high schools (for auditorium space), churches, synagogues, or local associations such as a Kiwanis Club.

Not unlike apartment hunting, you will want to visit each space that might potentially meet your needs to see if it is usable. Advertisements do not always give you the full picture—*including the ones with full pictures.*

Prior to seeing what is available, consider your own needs. For example, how large a production are you staging and how much space onstage and backstage do you require? A large musical typically needs a large theatre, with ample stage room to accommodate the show. Musicals such as *Oklahoma!*, *Showboat*, or *42nd Street* require plenty of room onstage, and backstage and can fill a large theatre, not only with patrons, but with sound. Of course, you could take a show like *Oklahoma!* and cast the five principals, with a few other cast members playing all the remaining parts. You can usually come up with alternative ways of making a show work.

An average-sized musical will be better served by choosing a mid-sized space. Artistically speaking, you need larger, more spectacle-driven shows in the big houses. A more character-driven musical with a smaller cast will work better in a smaller theatre.

Musicals like *The Fantastics*, with five people and a piano, are not likely to fill a thousand-seat theatre, but are ideal for summer stock theatres with three hundred seats. Musicals with small casts and small orchestras are perfect for regional theatre. A lot of the Off-Broadway revues are good for smaller theatres, such as Stuart Ross' zany revue *Forever Plaid*, Joe Dipietro and Jimmy Roberts' *I Love You, You're Perfect, Now Change*, Clark Gesner's *You're a Good Man, Charlie Brown*, or perhaps, Howard Ashman's offbeat musical *The Little Shop of Horrors*, based on the old Roger Corman film.

When you're not staging a musical, look for a smaller space to capture some intimacy with the audience. A dramatic piece would likely lose its impact in a thousand-seat theatre. There are other practical elements involved, such as the scenery needs of a full-scale musical. Small theatres cannot accommodate numerous set changes. Nor can they accommodate eighteen performers onstage at one time. Conversely, a massive stage with three performers on it may dwarf your actors, and your show may be lost somewhere in the vast surroundings. It's all a matter of fitting the right show into the right size theatre so that the audience feels connected. To illustrate the point, Steve Martin, while on tour at large venues, like the nineteen-thousand-seat Nassau Coliseum in Long Island, used to walk onstage and say, "And now I'm going to perform the disappearing dime trick."

Some of the best theatre you can see is found in the small theatre companies. In an intimate theatre with only ninety-nine seats, the audience feels like they are involved with the show. For example, at the Actor's Theater in Nantucket, I once directed an A. R. Gurney play called *The Golden Age*. It was perfect for that stage, which had about two hundred seats. It was a character-driven play, and audience members felt as if the characters were talking directly to them—they were part of the action. You can't get that sense of involvement or envelopment in a large theatre. In fact, most of Gurney's works are excellent for such small, intimate settings.

On Broadway, the smallest theatre spaces today are in the Booth and Helen Hayes Theaters, which hold six to eight hundred people. While not nearly as intimate as the ninety-nine-seater, such theatres are a good fit for smaller plays, including one-person shows.

Another factor to consider is where you will be located—or, as they say in real estate, location, location, location. While any theatre space in Manhattan that is considered to be "on," or "off" Broadway has a cachet to it and will draw (if the show generates decent reviews), out-of-the-way locations in New York, and in most towns and cities, make it harder to fill the house without significant (and sometimes costly) promotion. Even the completely revamped strip of small theatres on West 42nd Street in Manhattan, between Ninth and Tenth Avenues, took some time to draw theatregoers. Many New Yorkers needed convincing after several decades of enduring a seedy, downtrodden 42nd Street, that the area had finally reemerged.

You will find areas that are in the process of regentrification in most towns and cities. A new theatre may be a marvelous idea, but it can take time to draw patrons. Likewise, you'll have other concerns with out-of-the-way locations (even if they come very cheap). Parking, safety, and accessibility can all be factors. Unless the show is a huge hit and draws people regardless of its whereabouts, it is to your advantage to consider whether you are in a familiar location, one which people are comfortable visiting after dark. As they say, beggars can't be choosers, and sometimes your choices of theatre space are limited, but don't rent a space in an area that people will not find or may not want to find.

Turning a Profit

Whether you are paying performers or trying to raise money for charity, turning a profit is very often one of your goals. If your rent and your costs are very high, try to book a space where you can draw enough paying customers to come out ahead. Crunch numbers and determine that if you pay x for rent, you will need to charge y per ticket to come out ahead. Keep in mind that your prices need to fit your demographic audience. If the potential audience typically pays $20 for adults and $10 for children to see a local family show, and you find you'll have to charge $35 and $20, you may price yourself out of the market. Even on Broadway, where people are now familiar with $100 or $125 ticket prices for a musical, you would be taking a great risk if you posted a $180 ticket price.

Like anything, it's all about supply and demand, with prices being fairly well set at a going rate. However, when a show like *The Producers* was so much in demand that they were able to create premium seating, you could pay $250 for an orchestra seat in the fifth row center on a Saturday night. If the show's hot enough like a popular resort in a warm climate during the winter months, you can get away with charging the extra money. Of course, do not assume there will be such a demand. Wait until one actually exists before charging higher prices.

Also, when renting a theatre, factor in to your equation the actual stage time you need to move into the theatre, which includes moving in the set(s), hanging lights, setting up your sound system, and so on. This counts as theatre rental time as well. And don't forget time to rehearse on the stage with the set. Again, this is time you will need to pay for. Many times you can work out a deal with the theatre owner to rent the space for a cut rate and rehearse there for several weeks. They will often give you the cut rate because the theatre is not being used and, since you are the next tenant coming in, it's better for them to get some cash flow than to sit with a dark theatre. This is more common in Off-Broadway theatres.

A good show is only part of the formula for making money in the theatre. Watch your expenses closely and, if you are renting theatre space, make sure you keep a close eye on all other expenditures, such as paying the house manager, ticket takers, box office people, and so on. In nonprofessional theatre, you should be able to get volunteers to handle many of these tasks.

Reading the Theatre Rental Ads

The following are sample theatre rental ads from local newspapers and theatre websites. This will give you an idea of what you will be looking at if you go theatre hunting in the classifieds, or Web classifieds. These have been adapted from actual listings. (*Specs* is short for *specifics* or *specifications*.)

Specs for a small theatre

The brand-new ABC theatre is located at the site of the former XYZ playhouse. It has been TOTALLY remodeled: new seats, new lighting equipment, new carpets, new lobby, etc.

Specs
- Theatre dimensions: 26 ft. wide, 16 ft. deep, 18 ft. ceiling
- Seating: 48
- Full lighting and sound equipment package
- Central A/C
- Beautiful, spacious lobby with concession area
- Plentiful free, safe, easy parking
- Production rentals include five days for preproduction technical work and rehearsal
- CALL to arrange an appointment
- Street and valet parking

Specs for a similar theatre

Specs
- Large stage: 30 ft. wide, 22 ft. deep
- 16 ft. high ceiling will accommodate 2-story sets
- 85 high-quality built-in seats, expandable to 99
- Central A/C and heat
- 2 dressing rooms and staging area
- Separate newly remodeled lobby with concession area
- 2 separate restrooms in theatre and lobby
- Fully equipped with lighting and sound equipment
- Outside marquee
- Production rentals include one day for preproduction technical work, tech, and rehearsal

Lighting
- Lighting board
- NSI programmable memory controller
- 16-channel programmable lighting board
- 16 scene memory
- 2-scene manual control with memory that lets you store a cue and recall it when needed
- Bump buttons
- Programmable chase

- Chase-rate control
- 10 Fresnels
- 10 Lekos
- 4 (four) 6 x 12 Ellipsoidals
- Follow spot (optional)
- In-house technical director / lighting

Audio
- Sound board
- CD player
- Dual cassette deck
- Upright piano

Parking
- Parking lot in rear
- Street parking
- Public lot across street

Specs for a black box theatre

Studio J Rentals for Classes, Casting Sessions, and Rehearsals

Specs
- Dimensions: 16 ft. deep, 24 ft. wide, 10 ft. ceilings
- Seating: 42
- Black box—sets possible
- Seats on risers
- Booth equipment lighting: 17 dimmers—Leprecaun 24 channel board—20 instruments
- CD player—tape deck, 2 speakers (2 more available)
- Includes use of 2 dressing rooms—lavatory—green room
- Share concession and box office
- 2 outside showcases—1 inside
- Shared actors lounge upstairs
- Box office program available. $300 per run of 6-week show plus $1 per ticket
- Street parking + lot two blocks north

When discussing theatre rental, make sure you cover all the bases, including insurance. If, when discussing the ad with the owner or manager, you are not sure what some of the technical details mean, ask. Also make sure to inquire as to who handles the equipment. Do you bring someone in or do they provide someone? If so, how much extra does that cost? In some cases there may be union restrictions stating that union members must handle all equipment or the process of moving in and moving out of the space.

Always stay focused on meeting the requirements of your show. While you may have to cut some corners or make some minor adjustments to fit the theatre, you do not want to damage the integrity of the production. Some alterations you can make to fit the theatre might mean scaling down some scenery or losing some props. Early in my career, I lost one of the poker players in *The Odd Couple*. In some cases, you may need to lose a small role; however, you don't want to jeopardize the impact of the performance. Juliet needs a balcony, and without a large plant, *The Little Shop of Horrors* becomes *The Little Shop of Bupkiss*.

Unconventional Theatre Spaces

Unconventional theatre spaces, as noted earlier, can make a production unique. Circle in the Square, a theatre in Manhattan, has a long catwalk extending from the stage, which is also known as a thrust stage. The unconventional setting worked very well for the unconventional musical *The Rocky Horror Picture Show*. Such spaces promote greater intimacy, and smaller musicals, with limited scenery, often benefit from such closeness. But if you need to fly scenery on and off the stage, a thrust stage is much more limited.

If you are not finding theatre spaces within your price range or size requirements, consider some alternate sites. For example, the most recent Broadway revival of the musical *Cabaret* was performed in, of all places, an actual cabaret. This cut out the need to re-create a cabaret setting within a theatre and utilized a venue that otherwise would have been dark between 7:00 and 9:00 P.M., prior to the opening of the nightclub, which was at 10. You might get a low rate renting out a warehouse and setting up chairs for a production or using a room in a church, temple, library, or other location for a smaller show. In Scotland, the first national theatre in more than half a century swung into action just a few years ago with some interesting venues, including an unused glass factory and a docked ferry. The idea was to show that theatre can be performed in a wide variety of locations. Remember, it's okay to think outside the box, or in this case, outside the theatre, when seeking a performance space.

Building and Growing Your Show

It is very rare for anyone to start at the top. Other than perhaps a LeBron James—the nineteen-year-old high school basketball star who went right into the NBA with a multimillion-dollar contract—most of us, in any given profession, work our way up the ladder over time. There is a learning curve and growth period, and the same can hold true for a show.

It may be advantageous to launch a production in a small, ninety-nine-seat house with the hope of generating great reviews. By doing so, you can move to a larger theatre with a buzz about the show and a greater possibility of making a profit, or at least covering your costs. In fact, you can go from a small, black box theatre to a larger three-hundred-seat venue and eventually graduate to an eight hundred-seater if the show has generated very strong reviews and you are filling the house at your current seating capacity. Off-Off-Broadway shows look to make the move to Off-Broadway and Off-Broadway shows look to step up to Broadway if the show is doing well, *and* if the show can succeed in a larger house.

How a Show Gets to Broadway

Generating excellent reviews and growing from a smaller to a larger theatre space is essentially the route most shows take to get to Broadway. The show builds momentum by garnering good reviews in smaller markets outside of New York while not costing a fortune to produce. This growth process also allows for many script, costume, scenery, and casting changes to be made along the way. For example, we started off the musical *Princesses*, written by Cheri and Bill Steinkellner, with lyrics by David Zippel, at a small theatre in Connecticut. It then had a run in a large, beautiful, two thousand-seat theatre in Seattle, Washington. The small venue gave us an idea of how the show would play in front of a big house. Plus, it was far enough away from Broadway to make the necessary adjustments without the New York media reporting our every move. Reviews were favorable, but not great, so we took the show back to the drawing board, rewriting the book and some of the songs before putting it up again. This is how a show grows.

The process of getting a musical to Broadway can take seven years, or longer. It's a long growth period in which you continue to hone the show until you feel it is ready. You always want to put forth the best production possible, with a strong cast. To complicate matters even more, each time you pull a cast and crew together during this growth period, you are doing so knowing that some of them will leave for other commitments.

Once we have a show that we are pleased with, we return to New York and set up readings to generate backers and interest from the Broadway community. Even if all goes well, and there is enough financial support for the show, it is still difficult vying for theatre space. At best, we get on the waiting list for a theatre to open up. Of course, with a musical, we are always limited to theatres that can accommodate the size of the production—meaning smaller theatres, such as the Booth and Helen Hayes, are no longer viable and, in the case of a mid-sized musical such as *Princesses*, some of the very largest houses won't work either.

Once we get the green light, meaning a closing date for the show currently in the theatre, we start preparing (usually several months in advance) to move in and start rehearsals and then previews. Even then, and especially then, there is a tremendous amount of work to be done to bring a musical into a Broadway theatre.

Touring

Imagine having to find not just one viable space, but a dozen or more as you take a show out on the road. Much of the traveling schedule for most touring theatre groups (including a growing number of highly professional, well-packaged children's theatre groups) is not contingent on renting space, but on getting booked into local theatres.

Lining up bookings, and essentially building a tour, is commonplace for many such troupes, who cross paths moving from venue to venue. By attending booking conferences, such as the annual conference in New York City by the Association of Performing Arts Presenters, or regional conferences, as well as having an ongoing promotional and marketing campaign, directors of such touring companies work diligently to keep their performers onstage as often as possible. Theatre managers make it very clear what they have to offer, while touring companies directors know the needs of their shows and determine whether or not they will work in a given theatre. It is always beneficial for the producers of a traveling show to have sets that are easy to move in and out. In short, it's advisable to "travel light." The more self-contained a show is, the easier it can play anywhere. Again, the size of the show and the size of the theatre need to be congruent.

"Once we have a show block booked in Florida, for example, we'll try to book other shows around that," explains Terry Bortom, director, showman, marketer, and booker for The American Magic-Lantern Theater, a unique professional touring company that re-creates Victorian "Magic-Lantern Shows." The show, which combines pictures, comedy, and plenty of participation, is very easy to move in and out of any location, allowing Bortom more options. "I go to my database and contact other theatre owners or managers in the area who either couldn't afford us or were already booked previously, to see if they are interested. The goal is to build a small tour around the two- or three-day booking," he adds.

Some touring theatre companies stay on the road for months at a stretch, while others set a more sporadic schedule, sometimes revolving around seasonal shows. Bortom sees his most successful bookings in October and December, when Magic-Lantern Theater has their highly acclaimed Halloween and Christmas shows. The key is to know the show you are marketing and your demographics. Then you need to seek out all appropriate locales, which for some shows would include fairs and festivals. Typically, the pay for the traveling performers is either a flat fee or a combination of a flat fee and part of the gate, known as a *split*.

The largest touring companies taking Broadway shows out on the road will often rent theatres in various towns. These are generally theatres that have accommodated large productions in the past. Most cities have just a few choices, so space rental needs to be secured well in advance. In fact, most touring companies, large or small, try to have their schedule completely set up the prior year. This allows time for promotion and marketing, not to mention carefully mapping out the travel itinerary.

Assembling the Creative Team

My Own Mother!

Perhaps you are thinking of involving family members in your production in some manner. Well, think it through more carefully. While my wife, Bonnie, and I have worked very well together on a number of projects, sometimes, it's best to keep family members from getting too close to the action.

I learned a valuable lesson when I invited family members to a production I staged for backers at a country club on Long Island. I was raising money for the show *A Change in the Heir*. I thought that doing a presentation of the show at the country club might entice some of the members to invest in the show. To show some family support, I had my wife, kids, and parents there. In fact, I got my mother a seat down front in the first row so she could see everything going on and be a prominent guest for the evening.

My mother arrived and took her seat front and center. I gave a little speech and then went and stood in the back. I told someone working at the club to turn the air-conditioning off as soon as the show started; it was too noisy and no one in the back rows would be able to hear the cast.

They began the presentation, and not ten minutes into it my mother got up and walked out. My own mother walked out of my show. So I raced outside to see what happened, what could possibly have gone wrong, and she walked up to me and said, "It's getting awfully warm in there."

I said "Mom, please, go back in and watch the show." She returned to her seat. But I knew from then on that it was probably best to be careful about inviting family members to important presentations.

Just as one production will have a full orchestra playing the score while another uses a single keyboard to produce the sounds of numerous instruments, your creative team will also range from a full team to one person wearing many hats.

A Broadway production team for a musical will typically start with the producer and include the director, librettist, music director, composer, lyricist, choreographer, set designer, costume designer, lighting designer, sound director, makeup artist, general manager, and stage manager. Of course, this may vary depending on the show. A show with an orchestra will likely add an orchestrator, while a new version of an established musical will not need a composer or lyricist. And, if you are not doing a musical, you can eliminate the musical director and choreographer entirely. The following is a brief description of the responsibilities of the creative team members.

Producer

The producer is like the CEO of a company. He or she secures funding, watches over the budget, and oversees the hiring of the creative team (in compliance with the wishes of the director). The producer makes sure that the lighting and sound system are in working order and that the staff is on hand to run the theatre as well as hand out programs, work the box office, and so on. The producer secures the venue and makes sure that everything is set to run smoothly. He or she stays informed on all matters of concern to the show, and may or may not get involved in decisions made by other members of the creative team, depending on the show and the team. The producer's goal is to get the best possible team to stage the best possible production while staying within the budget, and for the show to be financially successful, which could mean a profit for investors or making money for a theatre company, charity, or school.

Director

The director is akin to the president of a company. It is his or her job to bring the show from the page to the stage. Through the dialogue, lyrics, dance numbers, and actions of the actors, the director is responsible for breathing life into the show. He or she is usually in charge of casting, and has control over the creative elements of the show. It is important to get a strong director. The best directors can usually find ways and means of taking something we've all seen and heard before and re-creating it in a new and dynamic manner.

Stage Manager

The stage manager, in the theatre, is akin to the vice president of the company. He or she organizes and coordinates rehearsals and makes sure that all necessary props and offstage equipment is in its proper place. He or she also serves as the liaison between the director and the various departments. In a professional setting, it is not uncommon to find a stage manager, deputy stage manager, and assistant stage manager. In nonprofessional settings there is usually one person handling the job. Other tasks of a stage manager include scheduling times for costume fittings, distributing changes to the script, cocoordinating "setup" and "breakdown" of the sets, calling all the sound and light cues for the show, and taking charge of everything onstage and backstage, from the arrival of the cast and crew until everyone exits after the production. In a pinch, stage managers have even taken over roles as understudies.

Clearly, this is a job for the most organized person you can find who wants to be involved in the production. It is not for someone who is shy, since he or she will have to communicate with everyone to make sure all is running smoothly on and around the stage. It is also not for a micromanager, since the various performers and crew members need to do their jobs without someone over their shoulders driving them crazy. A knack for scheduling and a take-charge attitude will serve your stage manager well.

Composers and Lyricists

Composers write the music and lyricists write the words. In most cases, this will not fall into your realm, unless you are staging an original musical, at which time you will look for either someone who does both, in the tradition of the legendary Irving Berlin or Cole Porter, or a team. Many times the impetus for doing a musical would come from marvelous musical teams, such as the Gershwins, Rodgers and Hart, Rodgers and Hammerstein, Lerner and Loewe, or the more contemporary Andrew Lloyd Webber and Tim Rice.

To transform a script into a musical, or an adaptation of a musical from another medium, match the style of the music to the time period and the tone of the show. Are you looking for music from the 1920s? Swing music from the '40s? Rock and roll from the '60s? Dare I say rap from the '90s? The composer and lyricist must fit the bill. Mathew Wilder wrote contemporary up-tempo music for *Princesses* that fit the bill, with fourteen teenagers in a production that is set in contemporary times. When we did *Thoroughly Modern Millie*, however, Jeanine Tesori wrote more classically oriented songs to complement the show, which was set in the 1920s.

Musical Director

For most amateur productions and musical revivals, this is the person who handles all musical responsibilites. Do you have someone with musical talent? Do you have someone who can work with your singers, patiently, to get the most out of each? Your musical director will determine who sings lead, who sings background, and in what key. He or she will work with—or may also double as— your accompanist for the show. "Tempo, people, tempo" are the frequently heard words of a musical director, who in many cases is the school's music teacher or a choir leader who has taken on the role by default.

If you are searching for a musical director for a specific show, seek someone who is familiar with the type of music in the show. Should you be hiring a musical director for a season's worth of shows, look for someone who can handle the diversity of several productions and several genres of music. A background in music plus some training in music written for the stage can serve you well; however, experience is often the best teacher.

Librettist

Also known as the *book writer*, the librettist creates the book (a/k/a the script) for a musical. While it is likely you won't need a librettist, it is a crucial role when presenting a new musical. The librettist has the job of bridging the songs and dialogue that move the story forward while engaging the audience. Some shows have such marvelous music that they can sustain a mediocre book. But many shows have failed because, despite a good score, the book was their downfall. *Guys and Dolls* almost never hit Broadway for this reason. Originally conceived as a serious romantic musical by producers Cy Feuer and Earnest Martin, the book was written and rejected eleven times by eleven different librettists before comedy writer Abe Burrows got hold of Frank Loesser's musical score and created a comedic version of the show. It was his comedic version that became one of the longest-running Broadway hits of the 1950s.

While the job is key, many librettists do not receive the same acclaim as other team members. For example, George Abbott is certainly not a household name today, but he did the book for *Damn Yankees*, *Pal Joey*, *A Tree Grows in Brooklyn*, and other hit Broadway shows. Betty Comden and Adolph Green, Moss Hart, and George S. Kaufman are a few in a long list of Broadway book writers over the years, a list that includes Ossie Davis, Truman Capote, and an uncredited Phil Silvers, who cowrote *High Button Shoes* with George Abbott. Only a few highly talented people have been successful as composer, lyricist, *and* librettist—notably as George M. Cohan and Noel Coward.

Choreographer

The choreographer puts the movement and dance into the show. For most productions, a dance director or dance arranger will do the trick, since there won't be a need for too many original dance steps. However, if you are working with a group of amateur teens, you may feel the need to create a few steps to that fit their MTV-style moves.

Look for someone unlike the musical director who has dance training or experience; someone who is comfortable with the style of dance that fits the show. If you have options, find a director of dance who specializes in a certain style. High schools, and certainly universities, almost always have someone who teaches dance. You can also look for the nearest dance school in your community and offer them free advertising in your program in exchange for their help.

The range of dance possibilities is quite expansive, from ballet to break dancing. Classic choreographers like Tommy Tune come from the school of tap-dancing choreography, while Bob Fosse introduced a jazz dance style that was both provocative and physically demanding. Through the past century and into the current one, Broadway has seen it all, from the early years of Julian Mitchell, choreographing large groups of dancers for Ziegfeld's musical revue, to the modern dance of Martha Graham, Twyla Tharp, and Alvin Ailey, to the latest from Jerry Mitchell.

Some dance background, a good ear for the music of the show, and plenty of patience will typically be the three primary qualifications for a dance director in an amateur production. It is his or her job to determine which dance numbers remain and which may be cut for the sake of time or difficulty. Is the dance number integral to the show? Does it move the story along? Clearly the dance representing the street gangs fighting in Jerome Robbins' *West Side Story* had a greater impact on the story than the dance numbers in Sherman Edwards' *1776*. It is easier to cut, or simplify, dance numbers that are not as integral to the story.

Going back to your initial selection of a show, know the talent level you have available. If you are working with an ensemble of talented dancers, show off their moves with a more dance-oriented show such as *Grease, Bye Bye Birdie, A Chorus Line,* or the recent revival of *Chicago.* Conversely, if your dance talent is limited and you have no choreographer, you can always select a "danceless" musical such as Stephen Sondheim's *Sweeney Todd* or Rachel Sheinkin's recent Broadway hit, *The 25th Annual Putnam County Spelling Bee.*

Note that choreographers typically handle other movement, such as a fight scene. Remember to work within the limits of your available talent, and be prepared to find creative ways to make action in a scene work, possibly with help from your lighting director or by using sound effects.

Technical Director

Just as your director brings together the cast and creative aspects of the show, the technical director is in charge of all things technical. He or she oversees whomever you have placed in charge of sets, lighting, sounds, costumes, props, and other related departments. The TD helps coordinate the purchase and delivery of construction materials and the installation of scenery, lighting, and so forth, into the theatre. In amateur productions your set, sound, or lighting director can double as your overall technical director. Like the stage manager, the TD should be someone who is well organized and can keep track of all that the tech crews need to be doing. Making sure that each crew has sufficient time and resources to do the job— plus creating a workable schedule—is part of the responsibility of the technical director.

Lighting Director

An often underappreciated role in theatre is that of the lighting director, who sets the tone for a scene through the creative use of lighting. The lighting director oversees all aspects of lighting for a production. This includes maintaining the equipment; designing, rigging, and focusing the lights; operating them; and taking care of all technical concerns. Ideally, he or she will be able to put together a lighting crew to assist in preparation for the production. A background in electronics and an understanding of the technical and safety aspects of the equipment is important when taking on this job.

Depending on experience, the lighting director, can do a lot with color and positioning. Given enough time prior to a performance, even a relatively inexperienced lighting director can experiment and come up with some interesting results.

If your location requires that you provide the lighting, your lighting director and/or crew will need to hang and position the lights. If this is the case, and you do not have anyone with a stage-lighting background, look for someone who is handy with wiring. The number one concern is safety, especially when rigging lights and keeping wires out of sight. The LD must also make sure the lights do not get too hot.

Controlling the stage lighting means either working the computer console or working the spotlight(s) manually. Find someone who pays attention to detail and who can follow the cues closely. In the event that you have several people available, one person can handle the technical aspects of setting up the lights and another operate them. In fact, in some cases, you'll find that you have someone with electrical know-how and someone else with some artistic flair. Utilize the talents of both.

Sound Director

The sound director, or sound operator, is responsible for the operation of the entire theatre sound system, including all onstage, and any offstage microphones as well as sound effects. Determining how many microphones are necessary and proper placement are vital. The sound director must also mike the performers, check sound levels, and eliminate feedback and interference prior to opening night. The bigger the production, the more difficult this job may become, since twenty or more people might be wearing microphones onstage at the same time.

The sound director controls the sound board, mixer, and all sound effects. The mixer output faders send the signal to the amp/speaker systems, typically from CD players or tapes. It is up to the sound director to select appropriate sound effects and to be prepared ahead of time, knowing the appropriate cues.

Not unlike the lighting director's role, this position calls for someone who is attentive to detail and good at multitasking. If you do not have someone with a background in sound technology, find somebody in the group who likes playing DJ at parties, or who has built a "monster" sound system at home. If you are fortunate, you will also have someone who has worked with microphones before. Enlist the talents of more than one person if necessary.

Your sound director or operator is also responsible for any public address announcements, which can include general announcements to the audience about not smoking and turning off all electronic devices, as well as announcements to the dressing rooms to let performers know they have five minutes to curtain. In addition, he or she typically handles the house music that proceeds and follows your productions. While it is a minor detail, remember that the house music sets the tone or mood of the production. When staging *In the Wings*, which was set in the 1970s, the audience listened to some top 40 hits from the '70s prior to curtain and during intermission.

Hint: Make sure that whoever is handling this job is very careful to label all sound effects CDs and tapes clearly, as well as the soundboard, so that each microphone level is easy to locate. Also remind your sound operator, or anyone working as a sound engineer, to place microphones on, and around, the stage *after* all sets are built to avoid dust and mechanical damage. Microphones break easily, so your sound person will have to take good care of them.

Wardrobe Coordinator or Technician

It is the job of the wardrobe coordiantor or technician to put together the various outfits that each performer will wear during the show. Each character should have a costume list that either comes with the script when you purchase the rights or is made up by you, the director, or the wardrobe coordinator. The job may also involve designing, sewing, and making alterations on costumes minutes before curtain.

Professional productions frequently have several people working on costumes, including a designer, who sketches out the fashions based on the time period of the show, the culture of the times, and the social class(es) of the characters. At any level, amateur or professional, research is necessary to determine the fashions and styles of the period.

The wardrobe team assists in maintaining the costumes and helping performers in making changes or reassembling costumes that may have become undone after a dance number. The wardrobe coordinator makes sure all costumes are gathered together after the production and ready for wearing during your next show. If costumes are borrowed or rented, he or she must see that they are returned.

Makeup Artists or Technicians

From eliminating unwanted shadows to transforming a perky eighth grader into the bride of Frankenstein, the makeup artist can play a key role in "the look" of your production. Along with enhancing the appearance of a character, makeup artists need to achieve continuity throughout the show unless, of course, the script calls for a character to have a different appearance throughout the production. In the play *Same Time, Next Year* the characters who meet every several years, are progressively older in each scene. Therefore, the makeup artist needs to continually alter their appearance.

Whoever is handling makeup for your production should work with each performer to try and match his or her skin tone and apply foundation accordingly. The makeup technician should remind actors to bring their own eye makeup and encourage them not to share, for health reasons. Your makeup artist or technician can then help apply eyeliner and mascara. For the most part, you'll want to impress on whoever is handling makeup that a little touch-up here and there can suffice—stage lighting and makeup together can create some unwanted appearances, so be careful. Prior to applying any makeup, make sure to inquire about allergies.

While most shows entail simply highlighting facial features, many shows for children will demand whiskers or other such features to personify animals or bring mythical and magical characters to life. It takes a good eye for detail to replicate some of the more unique characters that have taken the stage in children's stories, particularly those found in fairy tales.

In amateur productions, makeup artists often double as hairstylists, or simply help performers who take care of their own hair prior to the show. One way of getting a professional hairstylist on board is to trade an ad in your program with a local hair salon for some stylistic help.

Hairstyles vary with the time period of the show. The length, color, and shape can make a big difference in the appearance of your performers. Whoever is styling hair should be familiar with the styles and trends of the period so the show achieves authenticity. You may provide some photos from the time period—most of which are easy to find on the Internet.

A great book on stage makeup, simply called *Stage Makeup*, comes from Richard Corson and James Glavan, who penned the book in 2000. It has since became the bible of the industry.

Set Designer and Set Manager

Whoever is in charge of designing and managing your sets needs to ensure that all sets are built, maintained, and in place for each performance. Set design typically requires dipping into your budget, unless you are shrewd enough to swing deals with a lumber yard and a paint store, which I certainly recommend trying. An ad in the program may at least get you a discount.

Together with your director, sit down with your set designer and discuss the vision you and your director have for the show and see what your designer can offer in terms of making that vision a reality. Remember, you may need to compromise for practicality. While the set designer creates the sets, the set manager should work with the crew to make sure all sets are built, painted, and tested for safety prior to opening night.

Your set designer should have a creative flair and an understanding of the space, while your set manager should be organized and prepared to oversee the safekeeping of the set.

Bringing the Team Together

In 1957, a Broadway show opened that featured the music of Leonard Bernstein, the lyrics of Stephen Sondheim and the book by Arthur Laurents. It was directed by Jerome Robbins, who also choreographed the show with Peter Gennaro. With a creative team like that, your job as a producer can become that much easier. The show was *West Side Story*.

A good team is not only the gathering of key personnel, but the collaborative efforts and the creative ideas that result from having the right chemistry. Find the right combination of people to take your vision and make it a reality on stage. You may find yourself seeking a combination costume manager–makeup artist, or your set designer might have to double as your lighting director. Be flexible and work with what you have available. Look for skills that fit the position, but remember that the personalities and attitudes of the individuals you select will factor heavily into whether your team clicks.

Finding the Right Team

If you have a general idea of people you think would fill the necessary roles, you might make a short list in advance. In most cases, however, you will want to let it be known that you are planning to do a specific show and how you envision it. Spread the word. You never know who may know someone with experience in an area that you need to fill.

By spreading the word far and wide, you can find someone with

- experience in that area,
- the necessary availability,
- enthusiasm for the position, and
- enthusiasm for the production.

In situations where you have few available resources, you may need to go with whoever volunteers. Assign each volunteer a role based on whatever limited experience he or she may have. If nobody steps up as a good directorial candidate, you may want to take on the role yourself, since you have the clearest vision of the production.

Theatre is a team sport, and you need to remember that there is no "I" in team. Keep an open mind and always welcome ideas and input. Allow people to get involved, share ideas, and build on each other's contributions. If you are fortunate enough to bring in experienced team members, provide them with your goals and visions for the show, and let them do what they do best. Many creative ideas stem from a cohesive team. I have found this to be true on numerous occasions. For example, the lighting director will ask me, "How would you like it if I add a little more green over here, so it will look like there's a light shimmering off the swimming pool?" I'll say, "That would be great, I'd love that." And if you get suggestions that you don't like, they may spark other ideas. One of the most exciting thing about working in the theatre, at any level, is that it is a collaborative enterprise where you are actually bouncing ideas off one another all the time.

Putting on a production takes a lot of work, but it should be an enjoyable group experience. The right team can have a marvelous time creating a show together. When we did *La Cage aux Folles* on Broadway, Jerry Herman wrote the music and the lyrics, Harvey Fierstein wrote the book, Scott Salmon was the choreographer, the great Arthur Laurants directed, and everything came together perfectly. Everyone had the same vision for the show. While working on another show while on the road, I recall the composers and lyricists being more concerned about who got the better hotel rooms than about writing new songs for the show. Not a good sign. You want a team that is more enthusiastic about the show than the extraneous details.

A strong creative team can make a huge difference since so much depends on their efforts, their enthusiasm for the project, and their ability to pull together. When bringing a musical to Broadway, try to keep the team together as long as possible. People are always coming and going. So if you are producing shows for a theatre company, a touring company, or any ongoing group of performers, start building up your contact list, with names of directors, set designers, music directors, choreographers, and so on. Categorize your list by the type of shows they have done, or the type of music or dance in which they specialize. You might also take notes on who has worked well together in the past. The longer the list, the easier it will become each time you are putting together a team for your next production.

Making It Work No Matter What

Perhaps the greatest test of a creative team is how well they make adjustments on the fly. Numerous shows have seen rewritten pages, new dance steps, and revamped lyrics practically thrown onstage to performers during readings and previews. As a show evolves, changes are made continually and the creative team must be open to constantly revising, rewriting, and revamping a show until it reaches its full potential.

Sometimes a hit show is the end product of so many changes that nobody is quite sure whose input resulted in what. To give you an idea of how it all can come together, follow the story of Peter Whitty, who won a Tony in 2004 for having written the book for the musical *Avenue Q*. On his website (www.whitless.com) he explains that the first draft of the show—originally written for puppets—was tossed aside and a completely new draft was then written. Ultimately, the two drafts were combined into one. He adds that the creative team's visions were frequently at odds, and that when the show debuted Off-Broadway in 2003, "It reflected none of our individual visions, but used the best of all of them."

When producing an existing show, whether it is a musical or a play, your goal, and that of your creative team, should be to do justice to that show and to the playwright by sticking to the script as closely as possible. Logistics, nervous performers, monetary constraints, and various external factors that are out of your control will very likely alter your route slightly from the script to final production. For this reason, *compromise* and *flexibility* are two key terms that must be instilled in the minds of your team. Creative team members should be ready not only to handle their tasks, but to pitch in wherever necessary. Wardrobes will need last-minute adjustments, missing props will need to be replaced, understudies will need a crash course on dance routines, and an accidentally mangled microphone will need to be compensated for on the sound board. It is all part of what makes the theatre experience so exciting. Anything can happen, prior to, and even during, a performance. Your team needs to stay on their toes until the final curtain.

Time Lines and Schedules

No matter how finely tuned your time line is, sometimes, in the end, it doesn't matter. While it is not necessarily an *amusing* anecdote, the story of opening the show *Ragtime* in London proved that no matter how well you plan, fate sometimes intervenes. I produced a version of the Broadway musical *Ragtime* in London. But instead of the full-blown production, which had numerous, somewhat cumbersome sets, we did a much simpler, lighter version featuring the music from the show, much like the recent version of *Chicago* that played on Broadway. So, there I was in London with the whole family; the press was on hand and everything was ready for opening night. Not unlike Broadway, opening night in London is a big event. As it turned out, another event was to take the headlines. That same afternoon the war began in Iraq. By the next morning, nobody was thinking about theatre, and everyone's television sets were tuned to news of the war for days to come. We were nominated for two Olivier Awards (the British equivalent of the Tonys) for best actress and best musical, but it closed after a short run. Unfortunately, wars too often have the longer run.

The journey from initial concept to opening night can be a long one. As I mentioned earlier, it can take up to seven years to get a musical to Broadway. For a play, the gestation period is shorter, but could still be two or three years.

Theatre companies like to set up their schedule a year in advance so that the production team can be plotting and planning for upcoming show(s) while the current show is still running. I like to get started on a show as early as possible to get the best cast and crew members lined up before they commit to other productions.

A school production is typically put together in a matter of a few months. In a drama department, the structure of the course frequently presents the students with a built-in time line, starting at the beginning of the semester and culminating with a final production at the end of the semester. In other situations your time frame is be dictated by external factors that may be complicated, such as the need to raise money for a proposed project that has to be started by a specific date, or having the opportunity to perform a show at an upcoming festival. Regardless of whether you have a defined amount of time of not, put together a time line and stick to a schedule.

The four most significant factors in determining how long it will take to put a show together are:

- **Money:** Fundraising takes time and will inevitably push your entire time line and schedule back; however, without sufficient time to raise funds, you may have no use for a time line or a schedule.

- **Human resources:** The more people you have working on a project, the more quickly it can be completed. Of course, without clear leadership and a well-thought-out plan, more people can also mean more chaos. Make sure everyone knows their responsibilities and follows the schedule.

- **Size and scope of the production:** A show with five people, minimal props, and no orchestra will typically get into production much more quickly than a full-blown musical extravaganza like *Oklahoma!*

- **Where the show will be performed:** Do you need to find a theatre? If so, allow time for theatre hunting. If renting a theatre space, coordinate your setup and rehearsal time with with the theatre owner or manager. While this may not necessitate additional time, it will mean paying strict attention to your schedule.

On the surface, deciding on starting and due dates for a time line or scheduling meetings and other necessary preproduction activities seems relatively simple. But once you start taking into account all that needs to be accomplished in preparation for a show, you will soon realize that this is normally an arduous task. Coordinate with team members to gauge how long tasks should take and have your director give you a rough rehearsal schedule as early as possible. While the time line should remain a constant, the meeting and work schedules will be altered based on how the show is progressing.

Creating Your Time Line

Once you have chosen your show, found a venue, and set the date for opening night, the fun begins. Now it's time to start listing everything possible that needs to get done, from casting and building the sets to choosing the colors for the tickets. Everything needs to be accounted for and someone needs to be responsible for it all. Take your time making up this list so you don't forget anything. A time line should itemize when each piece of the production needs to be started and completed.

The following is a sample time line providing a rough overview of how you can proceed. Adjust it accordingly, based on the specific requirements of your show, the cast, and the crew. (The sample is for a musical; a play would typically be a little shorter.)

Sample Time Line

Dates are prior to the first preview:

6-Plus Months Out

- Select a show.
- Obtain rights to show.
- Put your budget together.
- List potential creative team members if you have specific people in mind.

■ Look for, and book, a theatre space if necessary.

■ Look for, and book, rehearsal space if necessary—remember, once you book a theatre, you may be able to work out a good deal for rehearsals since the theatre will be dark as your show approaches.

15 to 26 Weeks Out (4 to 6 Months)

■ Select your director.

■ Select your creative and production teams, including musical director and choreographer (if you are doing a musical); costume and set designers; lighting, set, and technical directors; stage manager; etc. Add your makeup artist and hairstylist later.

■ Hold initial meetings with the full team. Discuss: budget, overall vision of the show, set, lighting, costume, and other design needs.

■ Determine who will handle publicity for the show.

■ Set up due dates for production needs.

■ Establish a meeting schedule.

12 to 15 Weeks Out

■ Preliminary set sketches are due.

■ Preliminary costume sketches are due.

■ Preliminary prop list with details are due.

■ Discuss talent needs: begin preparing audition notices.

■ Prepare initial promotional advertisements.

■ Determine program advertising rates and begin program ad sales.

■ Find local printer or someone who has desktop publishing software and expertise.

■ Establish where auditions will be held.

10 to 12 Weeks Out

■ Director prepares sides for auditions.

■ Post audition notices.

■ Order materials for sets, costumes, props.

- Begin publicity campaign.
- Design program.

8 to 10 Weeks Out

- Hold auditions.
- Hold callbacks (within a week after auditions).
- Final set designs are due.
- Final costume designs are due (or list of what is to be bought, borrowed, etc.).
- Final prop list is due.
- If you haven't done so, add your hairstylist and makeup artist(s).
- Producer confirms rehearsal space(s), director creates rehearsal schedule.

6 to 8 Weeks Out

- First meeting of full cast; director should provide the concept and vision of the show.
- Director distributes rehearsal schedule—make necessary adjustments.
- Musical director and choreographer should provide their insights.
- Initial script readings with full cast.
- Publicity photos taken.
- Begin set construction.
- Preliminary sound cue list including sound effects and cues for preshow, intermission, etc.
- Cast measurements for costumes.
- Begin costume construction.

4 to 6 Weeks Out

- Preliminary lighting design outlined: This should include a floor plan showing the stage broken down into lighting areas, with color included.
- Preliminary sound design outlined; this should include where all mikes will go onstage and on actors.

- Review where you are in prop and costume construction— along with the director, you should look over the props and costumes you have to this point and determine what else needs to be made, purchased, or borrowed.
- Begin music and dance rehearsals.
- Begin blocking rehearsals.
- Begin poster designing and creating.

3 Weeks Out

- Cue sheets should be completed.
- Complete program ad sales.
- Complete final program design.
- Run through music with orchestra.
- Run line rehearsals (cast should be off-book).
- Complete final lighting design, including list of gels, etc.
- Complete final sound design, including director's sound cue list, microphone, and sound effect list.
- Hang posters in local businesses.
- Paint set.

2 Weeks Out

- Send final program to printer.
- Set should be completed.
- Hang lights.
- Rehearsals continue.

7 to 10 Days Out

- Review final props: Make sure everything is accounted for.
- Put sound system in place.
- Hold technical rehearsals.
- Costumes should be completed.
- Hold run-throughs

4 to 7 Days Out

- Hold costume parade (to see how actors look in costumes and what adjustments need to be made).

- Make costume adjustments.
- First dress rehearsals, should continue every day.
- Get programs back from printer.
- Do dry tech (this is a technical run-through of the play with the technical team, not the actors).

1 to 3 Days Out

- Hold final dress rehearsal, with makeup.

Your time line can be more detailed and include as many elements of the production as you feel are necessary. For an original play there will need to be sufficient time built in for changes to the script. For an original musical you will need more time to allow for changes to the music, lyrics, and book. When building a time line, allow enough time for all technical tasks to be completed and for cast members to explore their characters and rehearse the show. An original show is more difficult because you have nothing to use as a comparison; you will need time to let the show grow and evolve. Although there may never come a time when an original play or musical is considered "finished"—as evidenced by my own changes to the show *In the Wings* (which I began writing more than twenty-five years ago)—at some point the show must be ready for opening night. You can make changes up until, and during, previews, but once opening night arrives, all you can do is hope for the best. A little prayer doesn't hurt either. Be realistic in your planning and remember, Rome wasn't built in a day, nor was the set for Sondheim, Shevelove, and Gelbart's *A Funny Thing Happened on the Way to the Forum*, set in ancient Rome.

Making a Schedule

Along with the time line featuring start and due dates, you will want to work out different schedules. The schedules will include the many meetings that will take place during the months prior to your production, along with a technical work schedule. A rehearsal schedule for the cast and crew, as discussed in Chapter 8 (on rehearsals) will also be drawn up by your director. Schedules should be posted so that everyone knows when and where meetings and rehearsals will take place.

Remember that amateur productions employ talent who hold a wide range of day jobs and are on differing schedules. Try to get availability up front from all team members so that you can find common times when everyone can meet. Early evenings on week-nights, and some weekend afternoons may be your best bet. If possible, turn some meetings into inexpensive dinners by ordering pizza or having a pot luck dinner. If you have scheduled cast and crew members to pitch in on a project, such as making flyers and posters, make a party out of it. The experience should be fun and rewarding as you all work toward a common goal.

Among the many meetings that precede the opening of a show will be the initial "creative" meetings where concepts and ideas are discussed. It is here that your creative team can bring a new twist to an established show or help develop an original script into a full-fledged production. An original show will demand many more meetings of the creative team than an existing show. At some point, however, the script must be handed over to the cast members and technical crew. Of course, as most producers and directors will at-test, the creative process for a new show will continue right up to the opening curtain (and possibly beyond).

Production meetings may start off on a biweekly schedule, but they will typically increase as you proceed. All technical areas of the show should be represented on the schedule with necessary meetings and specific work days posted. Telecommunications can be helpful—including conference calls, which work for certain technical concerns—but face-to-face meetings are still a necessary part of the process.

To get the most out of meetings, whether they are creative or technical, draft a basic agenda in advance and stick to it. Remind your director and the heads of your various crews to do the same for their meetings. Make sure someone is taking notes, so that all clever, and not so clever, ideas are recorded for future reference. You'd be surprised at how often a mediocre idea sparks a better one somewhere down the road. Remember, all your meetings need to be purposeful, so you don't waste people's time. Don't get into the habit of meeting for the sake of it.

Following the initial creative and technical meetings where new ideas and developing concepts are paramount, your meetings will begin to focus on progress reports as work gets under way. This is where you will determine how each aspect of the production is evolving. In the course of being updated on the progress of the various technical and creative areas of the show, you will find that certain aspects of the show are progressing rapidly while others are lagging behind. It is rare that your director; your set, sound, lighting, and costume designers; and your musical director, choreographer, and publicist will all report that everything is right where it should be. Something will inevitably fall behind or hit a snag, and you will need to shift focus and give greater attention to those problem areas. You might need to ask others to pitch in and help. If, for example, you find that ad sales for the program are way behind your expectations, everyone may have to pick up the phone and help your ad sales team by making a few impromptu phone calls. Likewise, if your props supervisor is unable to come up with several items on the list, your cast and crew can certainly help out. These are examples of the camaraderie, or teamwork, discussed in the previous chapter. Even on Broadway, celebrities are asked to do promotion for a show, whether it's a commercial or an interview.

From the always important financial perspective, meetings should also allow you to keep track of your budget. You will discover where your budget covers, or even exceeds, specific needs, and where you need to allocate more funding. If, for instance, your costume designer has made a deal to get inexpensive fabric, saving you money, but your lighting designer needs several new gels to make a couple of scenes far more effective, then readjust the budget to reflect this change.

The ability to shift focus between the technical and creative aspects of the show is paramount for a producer. What begins as a creative idea for a show, slowly becomes a cut-and-dried technical process involving numerous people who set the stage and create the atmosphere that brings the show to life. At the same time, the creative aspect of the show continues and evolves with performers presenting the words and playing the music. As producer, you want to keep everything proceeding as smoothly as possible.

Your director should keep you apprised of the creative progress, and through your stage manager, you should be filled in on how rehearsals are going. Meanwhile, your technical director will keep you informed of all technical progress. For an amateur production, you can expect to be spending a lot of time in both camps, working closely with your creative and technical teams. While it keeps you busy, it is also extremely exciting to watch the show come together.

Murphy's Law of the Theatre

While *everything* that can go wrong, usually won't, Murphy's Law does have some application to the theatre: en route to opening night, several things inevitably will go awry. In the course of staging a show, cast or crew members may get sick, quit, storm off in a huff or end up at the Betty Ford Clinic. Sets will collapse, catch fire, or not fit into the theatre, while props and costumes will disappear, reappear, and disappear again. You may even find that your theatre space had been shut down for failure to pay back rent. Your job will be to correct such situations or find ways to work around them.

Over the years, I've seen everything, from props missing during previews to fire alarms going off the day before opening night (read Chapter 4, for more on that little episode). I once directed a show called *The Gig*, by Douglas J. Cohen, based on a movie by Frank D. Gilroy. A large carousel of sorts was built as part of the set, with three compartments, or cubbies, on top and three on the bottom. It was built to revolve, and on the other side there was a blank screen so you could project something onto it. In the three cubbies on the ground level, I planned to put hospital cots, with three others on the stage. For some reason the set designer could not locate these cots. A few days before previews he came up with three larger, aluminum cots. I asked him if he thought they would fit and he told me "absolutely." So I said "fine," and off he went to get them. I had choreographed the scene around the structure we had built. When the cots finally came in, two days before we were supposed to start previews, sure enough, they didn't fit.

"You told me they'd fit!" I could hear myself responding as my blood pressure went up a notch.

"I forgot to account for the thickness of the wood . . . a half inch on either side," replied the stage manager.

So I had to reconfigure the stage to fit these extra cots and rechoreograph the dance number around them. It was tight; we had six cots on stage. We managed to do the scene, but never used the set that was originally, and elaborately, built to accommodate them.

The problem is when you spend time solving one crisis, you sometimes have no time to attend to other problems that come up, which in this case were the sound effects, which had been recorded at different sound levels, so that each time the sound director hit one on the sound board it was a complete guess as to what level it would come in at. You'd hear a door slam at a low level and later a piercingly loud doorbell would ring. In the end, there was no time to rework the sound effects, so we cut them completely and panto-mimed doors slamming and whatever else we could.

When this type of thing happens, they'll forgive you at a pre-view or two, but once the critics come in and it's opening night, there's no forgiveness.

7

Auditions and Casting

Bernadette Peters is a wonderful actress, a real child of the theatre who shines whenever she's on the stage. She's dedicated, talented, and professional. We were doing *Gypsy* and it was exhausting; she was playing Mama Rose, a very demanding role. To make things worse, a lot of effort had to go into the show, with many changes involved. This meant more rehearsals, and Bernadette, a consummate professional, was always there, working very hard. As it also happened, with all the extra work, she started losing her voice, and for the good of the show, we had her take some time away from rehearsals. Naturally, some New York newspaper columnist latched onto this and started writing that Ms. Peters was being a diva and not showing up for performances when in fact, she was getting laryngitis and could barely speak, much less sing. Once the rumor mill gets started in this business, it's very hard to shut it down. Consequently, after *Gypsy* was up and running, and despite the fact that Bernadette Peters never missed a performance, people still asked, "Is she still in the show?"

"Next!"

The process can be long and arduous, but the results of casting can make or break a show. The right actor can bring a mediocre show to life, while poor casting decisions can turn a classic gem into a classic disaster. Casting is more than simply finding talent, it's finding the right fit for the roles you need to fill. It's having a vision of a character and finding that special someone who matches your vision. In some cases you will discover a talent who can bring something extra to a role, while in other cases your director will need to work long and hard to fit a square peg into a round hole.

The casting process can lead to surprising discoveries. When we were casting our lead for the Broadway production of *Thoroughly Modern Millie*, our initial choice for the role was Kristin Chenoweth. Kristin, however, had her sights set on Hollywood, so she declined and we held auditions. After looking at numerous potential Millies, we made a decision and thought we had our leading lady. But just when we were set to open, our Millie took sick and her understudy, Sutton Foster, was forced to step in and take over. As we watched Sutton onstage, I still remember hearing Michael Mayer, our director, exclaim "That's our Millie!" Sutton laid claim to a role that she would remain in for the life of the show.

Of course, such a story is not new to show business. Perhaps the most famous example of rising to the occasion was the story of Shirley MacLaine, who got her first role because the lead actress broke her leg.

Casting is far from an exact science, but there is a method to the madness. Depending on the group staging the performance, the show selection, the budget, and a wide range of other factors, you'll find yourself making your casting decisions for a variety of different reasons. In this section, we'll take an overview of casting.

Limited Choices

When casting within a school or community theatre group, you are limited by the number of performers and the talent level available. The possibilities of casting certain types will often dictate the show you select. Prior to auditions, you may have a certain character type who would be perfect for a specific show. For example, an all girls' school with a talented little redhead might prompt you to do *Annie*. Often, the idea is to build a list of possible shows based on who is interested in performing, rather than trying to do a show for which you will have to look long and hard to find the types necessary. Of course, you could also be daring and go against the type. There was a female version of *The Odd Couple* that hit Broadway starring Sally Struthers and Rita Moreno. It garnered some favorable reviews. But this type of counterproduction can be a gamble, the results of which can be very entertaining or a complete disaster. So be careful.

While you won't find a play that fits each of the dozen types in your ensemble, look for a show for which you have at least a couple of potential leads at your fingertips.

To round out any production with a limited number of players, you can, and will, need to use some imagination. For example, the musical *Princesses* is based in a contemporary girls' school where the students are putting on a theatrical production of the 1939 film *Little Princess*. The script calls for some of the girls to play the male roles. A shorter girl plays the leading girl's brother, while a taller girl will don a mustache and be her father, and so on. There's a song in the show called "What a Drag," about three of the girls who are tired of always being asked to dress in drag or don mustaches to play male roles. In community theatre, and certainly in school shows, it is not unusual to find someone playing a cross-gendered role. In a comedy, that alone can sometimes add to the laughs.

It should be noted that this concept is far from a new. In Shakespeare's time, men played all the female roles. Even today, the Grand Dame is always played by a man.

While you typically seek out specific types, many roles can be filled by a variety of talent. Curly, in *Oklahoma!* need not be a specific type; in fact, he doesn't even need to have curly hair. You can try for authenticity, but there will be limits. I recall being in a school production of Howard Lindsay and Russel Crouse's *Life with Father*, and the teacher tried to re-create the effect she had seen on the Broadway stage where the entire family—the father and his three sons—all had flaming red hair. She said, "Okay, you kids are going to dye your hair red, right?" We all looked at each other. While I was willing to do it, the other actors were not as committed to their art as I was. So much for authenticity.

If you're looking to stage a musical, you'll need to see who can sing, who can dance, and who can act. It's rare to find all three in one person, known as a "triple threat." If you do, you've probably got your lead. Whether you're working with a limited group or having open auditions, you may find certain people who are very strong in one of the three areas, or perhaps two. Don't let these people slip through the cracks.

To incorporate your best singers and dancers into the show, spread the lead role around a little. Cast the strong actor in the lead, but cast the best singer in a secondary role and give him or her the key songs. Have your strong dancer as a secondary character who can do the dance routines that might otherwise have been done by the lead. This keeps the song and dance numbers in the show without forcing the talented lead actor with two left feet and a mediocre singing voice to try and hit the high notes and learn to dance. By utilizing good actors, singers, and dancers in such a manner, the show is much stronger and the choreographer and the musical director are happy. Plus, the audience gets the full experience of the show, even if it's not all from one person. Too often, producers or directors seek one person with all three talents or try to mold someone into a triple threat. Most of the time they fall short and the audience is disappointed. Don't try to create something that may not be there; go instead with the strengths of the people you have.

Open Auditions

For any show, whether in a school or a major theatre in your town or city, auditions are part of the process. Open auditions typically start with a casting call in a local theatrical paper. They can also begin with well-placed signs or posters in a school or around the community.

The goal is to let it be known that you are seeking talent for a show. Start out by making it very clear when the performance(s) will take place. The last thing you need is to find a wonderful talent who can't make it to opening night. Of course, if the talent is so terrific that you can't let him or her get away, you might change the performance schedule. Even Broadway shows have opened or closed later than anticipated to accommodate a star, although this is not the usual approach. When posting audition announcements, include:

- the name of the play and the playwright;
- a brief description of the play;
- the time, place, and location of the audition (You may want to hold auditions at a couple of different times to accommodate a wider range of potential performers. For example, a community theatre may have one audition on a weeknight and one on a Saturday afternoon. At a university, since students have very different schedules—even in the same department—you might have one audition during a weekday afternoon and one on a week night);
- when rehearsals are expected to begin;
- the date or dates of the production;
- the location of the production; and
- if applicable, whether the play is a union production; and
- what to bring to the audition, including where to pick up the script or specific material for the audition, unless you are allowing them to select their own audition material. Make clear what they are or are not expected to do.

Audition Forms

You should also have an audition form prepared in advance, so that you have everyone's information readily available. This should include name, address, phone numbers, special skills, acting or onstage experience, and any other basic information you may think is necessary. At a university, you might ask what year the student is in, or whether he or she is part of the drama department. You should also include a line explaining that casting decisions are made at the sole discretion of whomever you choose (director, director and producer, teacher, etc.). This sheet should be signed and kept with the resume and headshots of the performers, if they have them. In community theatre, schools, and other local shows, such as those presented by associations, corporations, or church or temple groups, it is unlikely that auditioners will have headshots, so this form may be the only data you have to refer to after the audition process. Attach your notes so you can easily distinguish one actor from another. After seeing twenty-five people—all trying out for the same role—you can be fairly certain they will all be one big blur by the end of the day.

Prior to posting audition notices, make sure any rules regarding the audition process are printed and handed out, such as when actors can expect to hear about a possible callback, where to leave headshots and resumes when they enter, and so on. Try to make the process as smooth as possible and start with enough time to see a number of performers. Also, remember to take breaks along the way—it's not fair to audition someone for a role when you are too tired to judge them appropriately.

You can also hold what are called "closed" auditions, where actors sign up to audition at specific times. This method is often used in a school or university, because it allows students to fill in a time that best fits their schedules. If you use this means of auditioning, try to stay close to the schedule; don't wait if someone is late for their appointed time. You can fit them in when it is convenient, but keep the process moving along.

If You Don't Know What You're Looking for, How Will You Know When You've Found It?

When auditioning actors, it is up to you to know what you are looking for before seeing talent. Have a clear description of each character. Read the script carefully. Know the show, know the characters, and determine what you want for the role. The description of the character should be inclusive and clear. Include:

- the physical characteristics: tall, short, hefty, etc.
- approximate age: 25ish, 18 to 20, etc.
- personality: shy, cranky, boisterous, etc.
- necessary talents required: improv, vocal range if required to sing, type of dancing if there are dance numbers, etc.

If you have a framework from which to start, you can get creative and find someone who doesn't exactly fit the description, but could lend something interesting to the character.

Casting notices may appear as follows:

Fagin: Male, lovable rogue, early forties, baritone, extremely agile, charismatic, with dark sinister qualities.

Tina: Bride, twenty to thirty, Italian American party girl, pretty yet tough, real New York prototype.

Laura: Late twenties, delicate, shy girl, fragile and socially awkward, self-conscious, has a potent internal longing that most can't see, more in touch with the world around her than many would imagine.

Vanna: Female, mid-thirties, blonde bombshell, out of Kim Novak / Jayne Mansfield mold, hard demeanor masks genuine vulnerability, sense of humor, superb high belt.

Steve: thirties, Stanley's poker buddy, husband of Eunice, brutish, hot-blooded, physically fit, abusive husband.

Some notices are longer and more detailed than others. Depending on the significance of the character, you can be more or less specific. Lead roles should be more carefully defined. For the leads, you will want to get as close to what you are looking for as possible.

If you have a large pool of potential performers, such as the entire city of Chicago, you'll want to be a little more specific when describing the type to limit a flood of responses. If, however, you are limited to a small student body, you may be more general in your descriptions.

Should you be auditioning talent for a troupe and plan to do several shows, look for range of talent and versatility. You may do four or five different shows and will need performers who can handle various genres. Try to cover as wide a range of types as possible with the few people you chose.

Taking Notes

Take notes that are meaningful to you. There is no "scorecard" or strict manner of evaluating talent. Everyone has his or her own system. As long as you know what is written down and what it means, your system is working just fine. You can simply take notes on:

- personal appearance, height, size (hefty/slim), hair color (at the moment), any distinguishing features that stand out
- ethnic appearance, types they could play or multicultural
- approximate age or age range, (e.g., nineteen to twenty-three)
- the song they sang
- the monologue they read

- specific abilities, such as taps well, good comic timing, great belt (for singers)
- someone they look like, such as young Jack Nicholson type (if you're lucky)
- ratings, such as Dance 10; Looks 5

Notes can be very simple; for instance

- raw talent, needs direction
- too strong for the role, may be good for something else
- great character type, not a lead

"Can't act. Slightly bald. Can dance a little." These were the notes of a 1920s studio executive following Fred Astaire's screen test. So remember, don't discount anyone, they may surprise you.

The idea is to take simple notes that identify the strengths or weaknesses of the many people you see. You want to be able to look at the notes with the headshots later and differentiate the good dancers, singers, and actors from one another and the potential leads from character types or supporting-role players. Keep in mind that someone with talent may not fit your current needs, but might be right for the next show you are planning to do. Find a few people for each role and think about understudies, especially in a school or community environment, where anything from poor grades to a sudden business trip may pull someone out of your show at the last minute. Hang on to your notes for future reference.

Make sure your audition space allows each performer enough room for dance steps or stage movement and provides you with a well-lit place to observe talent. Seek out a location with good acoustics and limited distractions. This means having a separate waiting area for actors who will be auditioning later. While many audition spaces offer nothing more than the bare essentials, you do not want anything to detract from your ability to evaluate the performer in front of you.

Be polite and respectful to each actor who auditions. They are nervous, and you need to be sensitive to that. By politely saying, "You're not right for this part" or "You're not quite what we're looking for" or something to that effect, you can make your point without hurting anyone's feelings. Thank each person for coming in. Remember, someone you pass on today could be ideal for another show, so be courteous.

Whose Material Should They Read, Anyway?

When I'm doing specific casting for one show, I have actors read from the script. I give them sides and let them have ten minutes to prepare. Sides are cards with the last few words of the previous line followed by their lines. Sometimes it's possible to get material to actors in advance, particularly if it's a school audition. In the case of an open call, have sides prepared when they arrive.

If you want to see the actors' overall level of talent, such as when casting for a season, you should let them prepare what they are going to do at the audition. You might ask if they can handle Chekhov, do *The Philadelphia Story*, handle comedy, and so on. The greater the range of talent in your troupe, the wider your selection of shows.

It's the same with music. You'll want to give them an idea of the style, then want to see what they can do. For example, you may be using a rock score, so you'll want them to come in with something appropriate.

If they bring in their own material, decide whether you want something you've heard before or something original. There are two schools of thought: A reading of something familiar gives you a frame of reference. Conversely, if forty people come in and do the same material, you may begin comparing one to the other, and it can become rather difficult to differentiate between the actors. New York casting agent Liz Lewis adds, "It can be refreshing if someone comes in with a piece their friend wrote for them or a passage from a novel that has some bite to it. It's nice to see someone come in with something different."

Creative Casting

There are certainly shows that have been built around stars. Liza Minnelli in *The Act* was a perfect example. You may have someone in a theatre group who has the physical look or abilities that remind you of a particular star. For instance, if you've got a Yul Brynner lookalike with talent, you might opt for Rodgers and Hammerstein's *The King and I*. This, however, is not a common scenario.

Utilize local star power in featured roles. Even on Broadway there are instances where secondary roles are created or altered to include a celebrity as a means of drawing media attention to the show. For example, when we put Marla Maples in a featured role in *The Will Rogers Follies*, on Broadway, the press turned out in droves. It lit a fire under the show, which had been running for some time. Not only did she draw prurient interest because of who she was, but she was quite good—although it took some work. In the end though, it was worth it.

You can attract similar media attention at any level. The local press will likely turn out to see a local celebrity or community leader doing a short stint in a secondary role in your show. In a school production, a teacher, guidance counselor—even the principal or dean—can boost your attendance. In a production of *Grease*, for example, why not ask the school principal to play the school principal or the gym teacher to play the gym teacher in a show that is otherwise performed by the students? Sometimes it's the out-of-the-ordinary casting that generates attention—as long as it's within reason and limited to one or two roles.

Callbacks

Most times, if you like what you see, you'll want to bring someone back and have them read again. A director will want to see specific emotions in the reading and ask an actor to read in such a manner.

By setting up various situations, you can see how your actors interpret the roles. What do they bring to the role? Sometimes the performers need to see the role performed. If you're doing *My Fair Lady*, you'll want them to watch Rex Harrison in the role of Henry Higgins. If you're doing *Cabaret*, you'll want them to see Joel Grey in the role of the MC. In some cases, you can provide more than one interpretation of the same role. For example, Alan Cummings re-created the same Joel Grey role in *Cabaret* more than thirty years later. The idea is not to ask the performer to try and replicate the talents of a Rex Harrison, Joel Grey, or Alan Cummings, but to have a frame of reference. From there, you'll want the performer to make the role his or her own. This is the actor's opportunity to show what they can bring to the character.

Anyone directing performers should learn the proper manner and language to use with actors in order to elicit certain responses. Books on directing, such as *Directing Actors* by Judith Weston, can prove very beneficial. Even nonprofessional performers can respond more easily when cues are specific. Make sure your director (which may be another hat worn by you) is not vague when trying to elicit a response. Set up the scene clearly: *You're at a dinner party with friends. You get a phone call and learn that your sister was seriously injured in a car accident. You're obviously upset and must leave immediately.* This sets up the scene clearly and allows the performer to react.

During the callbacks, your director can also get a feel for how the actor takes direction. It is expected that the director will have to work with performers to get the most out of them. At the callback you can get a greater sense of the actor's ability to commit to the role.

By the second or third callback, both the director and producer are also looking for chemistry. You want to see how the actor interacts with other people.

- Do they work well together?
- Is the chemistry right?
- Do they look right together?

Height, hair color, size, shape, speech, everything needs to be taken into consideration. She's blonde and blue-eyed, he's got red hair—will they contrast? Will they look right together? Do they look like a family? Does someone stand out or appear out of place?

The interaction and the chemistry between performers becomes a significant part of the process at this stage. Sometimes it's a matter of minor adjustments in wardrobe, makeup, or other physical aspects that are easy to change. In other situations, you can have two great performers, but if there is no chemistry between them the project falls flat. You want lovers to react to each other with passion, and sworn enemies to elicit the hatred they have for one another. In comedy, it is particularly important that performers come in at the right moment with a punch line and do not step on each other's lines. Directors will work with performers, but you need to watch that they are convincing together in whatever relationship they are supposed to have onstage.

In 1983, we had longtime song and dance man, Gene Barry, along with George Hearn in *La Cage aux Folles*, and didn't know how they would work together. It was a different show than either had ever done before. They were both convincing in their roles, but would it click when they were on stage together? They turned out to be terrific, the chemistry was great. It is exciting to take chances and see if it works. That's why theatre is so magical, and casting, as I said at the beginning, is not an exact science.

Some Considerations When Casting

- Have one final decision maker. This should be the director. If several people are involved in the audition process, the director will make the final call. Of course, as producer, if you land a local celebrity, you will need to work with your director to fit him or her into a role.

- Don't forget about understudies. These should be cast members already in the show. They should take some time to learn the roles of the leads and be prepared just in case. In some instances, crew members or your stage manager may be able to fill in for some of the smaller roles.

- In school productions or community theatre there is a tendency to put the performers in roles similar to those they have handled before—to make the casting process easier. Such situations do not allow other performers to have leading roles, nor does it help teach an actor how to fully use his or her craft.

- Don't underestimate the value of stage presence and likability. While you may not always find the talent level you are hoping for, you may find a would-be performer with great stage presence and a demeanor that draws attention. While this person may be better suited to be spokesperson or game show host, your show can get a boost by having such instantly likable cast members.

- Keep diversity in mind. While shows may call for one ethnicity, you can and should make an effort to bring in ethnic and cultural diversity.

Rehearsals and Previews

Be Careful What You Write

Like most directors, I take notes when directing a show. At one rehearsal I left my notes on the stage when I took a short break. One of the actors apparently just "happened" to get a glimpse of the notes I had written. When I returned and started talking to the cast, I could see that the actor was quite nervous. Approaching me, he said he was very concerned about having to do a Polish dance. He didn't know any Polish dances and had no idea how to do one.

A bit confused, I explained that I had no idea what he was talking about. Then he confessed that he had looked at my notes and saw that I had written "Polish dance" next to his name. I replied, "It says *polish* dance, as in make it better!" He was greatly relieved and I learned never to leave my notes in view of the actors.

To rehearse is defined as "the act of practicing in preparation for a public performance." To that end, we schedule plenty of rehearsals. It is during rehearsals that the cast and crew will present and, yes,

97

polish their respective talents and abilities while learning their roles, onstage and backstage. For the director, rehearsals provide an opportunity to shape, mold, modify, alter, adjust, and even transform a group of individuals into a cohesive unit. For a producer, it is an opportunity to see whether his or her vision for the show is coming to fruition.

At all levels, whether the actors are honing their skills for a future in theatre, raising money for charity, engaged in a labor of love, or earning top dollar on the stages of Broadway or London, the desire to shine on stage is inherent in all performers. For that reason, coupled with the desire of the producer, director, cast, and crew to provide the audience with a worthwhile experience, the rehearsal process can be quite demanding.

A director sets the pacing of rehearsals, in essence steering the ship toward its final destination, the vision he or she has for the show—in conjunction with the producer's vision of course. As a director, you have to look at the whole picture and see the production from beginning to end. Actors will take the show from moment to moment, from scene to scene. The director has to have a wider view—to understand the tension, the momentum, and pacing of the work; to see where the show builds in intensity and moves the story forward and where it is simply treading water. A director must anticipate where the scene is going and see if the actors are staying on course or if they've lost the vision somewhere in the last scene.

When I direct a show, I like to get it on its feet right away and physically stage it as soon as possible. Then I go back and discuss the characters—why they did certain things or responded in a certain manner. The actor should give the line the way it is written; any questions should be answered right there in the text. If the actor is having problems and does not understand something in the text, then he or she can ask why the character acts in such a manner. If it's an established play, I'll explain the history behind it. If it's a new play and I don't have the answer, I'll go to the playwright. A proven play is easier to direct because you know it's good and people like it. Even so, it's important to bring something new to an established show that people have seen many times before. A new play is more difficult to direct because everyone's doing something for the first time and nobody is quite sure how it will work. While exciting, doing a new show also brings a greater degree of risk, since its success has yet to be proven.

As a producer, you will get daily reports of the rehearsal process from the stage manager. Look to see if the concept is working. If, for example, you see that the director has characters flying through the air and it's a courtroom drama, you will want to sit down with the director and say, "I don't quite understand what you're trying to say with this." Unless something is moving really far away from the original vision that you and the director initially shared, though, maintain faith in your director to come up with new visions and new ideas.

Since schedules are often tight, you will also want to see that the show is moving forward. When three weeks of rehearsal have passed and you start hearing from the stage manager that for five days the director has done nothing but sit around the table and talk about characters, a red flag should go up. Clearly, it's time to get the show on its feet. Some directors like to spend a lot of time sitting and talking about motivation. But that is really the actors' job. There's an old story in the theatre about the famous director, producer, and writer George Abbott, who was directing a show. At one point he told an actor to go to the other side of the stage. The actor stopped and asked, "Mr. Abbott, why am I going over there, what is my motivation?" To which George Abbott replied "your paycheck."

It's a good story because it reminds actors that they can get caught too caught up in detail, as can directors or even producers. The director has a vision; if he says you should go over there, you should go. The actor, meanwhile, should be working to come up with his or her own motivation as to why. As director or producer or both—in the event you are wearing two hats for an amateur production—it is to your advantage not to have all the answers readily at hand, but to make your actors work and explore. You want them to find motivations and answers to questions about their characters for themselves. This is how the creative process grows and how actors explore and experiment with a character. If you tell them exactly how to do everything, they will never dig deep down and use their own creativity. This can be a shame, because something marvelous may be lurking inside. I recommend that actors do their homework and seek motivation while they are familiarizing themselves with their roles.

During rehearsals, as director and even as a producer, have enough faith in your actors and all the artistic people involved to encourage them to try new and different things. You may want to see someone get more radical with a particular character or try something unexpected. By encouraging performers during rehearsals, you can discover new, exciting, and funny things that may enhance a performance.

Rehearsal is an exciting process because you get all the input—from the actors, costume designers, lighting designers, set designers, choreographers, and everyone else. You'll watch the show emerge throughout the process, until it becomes the production you envisioned.

Establishing a Rehearsal Schedule

When setting up a rehearsal schedule, it is important first to understand the general path rehearsals will take, starting with the initial orientation or meeting to introduce cast members to one another and to discuss the script and vision of the show. This is usually the job of the director.

At this initial gathering of cast members, it is wise to start out with introductions (unless they have worked together in a company before) and all the basic guidelines. This can include anything, from policies for lateness to where to park and hang up jackets. As producer, you may help your director establish a list of dos and don'ts, unless the director comes prepared with a printed handout. As long as everyone knows the ground rules of rehearsals, everything that follows should be easier—but don't count on it.

The next step is handing out the script, at which point everyone will look at the pages and nobody will be paying attention to anything the director says. Allow a few moments for script browsing, then call for a discussion. Producers may or may not be involved at this point, depending on the nature of the production and the director's preference. Usually, in theatre, there is no hard-and-fast rule. When staging a familiar show with experienced performers, the producer typically has no reason to be present. If, on the other hand, you are dealing with an original script, new talent, or a new director, you may want to be available to explain your vision and lend your support.

Next comes a read-through of the script. While the director should be aware that most of the actors are unfamiliar with the material (even in an established show, actors can not be expected

to know it line by line), he or she can get an idea of the performers' understanding of their respective roles. During a read-through,
the director will explain aspects of the play that the performers may
be missing or misinterpreting. The read-through also allows the director to discuss his or her vision of the show, answer initial questions about character motivation and interpretation, and help
actors understand how their characters fit into the overall scope of
the show. Depending on the show, the size of the cast, and their
stage experience, the read-through can take one or more days.

Blocking Rehearsals

After read-throughs, rehearsals move onto the blocking phase. *Blocking* is a term derived from Greek theatre, in which actual blocks were
placed onstage to determine where the actors would stand. Today
it means the movement that the director gives the actors. In the
blocking rehearsal, the director tells the actors where to move
throughout the play. This includes entrances, exits, and various
positions during the show. Many directors preplan their blocking.
For the actors, blocking provides a more realistic, physical aspect of
their characters beyond just their lines.

Line Rehearsals

Line rehearsals follow. This is the time in which actors are required
to learn their lines. Directors approach this in varying manners,
depending on their own style and the book the actors are trying to
learn. The script may be divided up so actors work on one act at a
time. A good director will notice which actors are learning lines
quickly and which ones are struggling, and pay extra attention to
those who are having trouble. Sensitivity to the fact that some actors
simply learn lines at a faster pace than others is important to remember at this point. Sometimes pairing more experienced actors with
newer ones can help the newcomers, provided the chemistry is right
between them. Directors apply various techniques to help actors
through the process of learning their lines.

During this stretch, directors also help actors with details that
need improving and show them ways to better understand their

characters, like exploring the subtext or intention behind the scene as opposed to just looking at the words they are saying. They may discuss how the scene advances the story or how the character grows by discovering something about himself or herself. Some directors have "calls," where specific scenes, or a portion of a scene, is rehearsed with only the actors involved. A director can schedule rehearsals for only those actors needed for a specific scene which eliminates the need to have twenty actors standing around while working with only two or three.

Motivation, interpretation, and the pacing of each scene are all watched closely and carefully considered by the director during this time period. Actors should be encouraged not only to learn their lines, but, as mentioned earlier, to explore their characters—how they move and speak, even their gestures and facial expressions. Many directors teach improvisational exercises or theatre games to help actors along; for example, giving one actor an assignment to get out of the room and another actor the assignment not to let the other person leave the room, without getting physical. This will last for a designated amount of time. There is a sense of urgency created as the actors work toward their respective goals. Marsha Norman's play *'night Mother* is similarly constructed. In the play, the daughter tells her mother that she is going to kill herself at a certain time during the show. The mother has to do whatever she can to stop her before time runs out. Another acting exercise is to have actors convey an idea by speaking only gibberish. There are numerous exercises used by directors to help actors prepare for their roles.

Run-Throughs

A run-through is a rehearsal in which all the elements of the production are put together in their correct sequence. Once again, as with many aspects of theatre, run-throughs are not set in stone. Some directors will have run-throughs at the end of each week to see the progress that has been made. Other directors schedule run-throughs only in the final two weeks. Run-throughs are the time for plenty of note taking. Directors take notes on anything and everything that might need fixing have the stage manager or assistant director take notes as they watch the rehearsal. Run-throughs include all elements of the production, and can point up areas that need work, from music coming in too soon, to lines being delivered too slowly. Following run-throughs, directors can also get the impressions of the actors and team members, who will notice things that the director may not see. Post-run-through meetings can be very useful for this purpose.

Technical Rehearsals

While your cast members are working hard to morph into their characters and learn their lines, your technical crew is also busily working toward a smooth, flawless production. "Tech week," as it's often called, is where all the technical aspects of the show come together. Two technical rehearsals, called "Dry" and "Wet" Techs generally take place at the start of that final rehearsal week.

Dry Tech is a rehearsal in the theatre in which you will hold your performance(s). The technical crews set up and run through all the cues necessary throughout the show. Every light, sound, and set change should be included and recorded (usually by the stage manager) in the Dry Tech. For a large-scale musical, or a complex production with many cues, this process can be quite long, lasting a number of hours. This is usually scheduled to start rather early on a weekend morning and includes a few breaks along the way.

Wet Techs are essentially full rehearsals with cast and crew. However, the emphasis is on the technical aspects of the show. Sound directors want to make sure the actors are being heard through their microphones and all sound effects are cued properly, while lighting directors want to make sure that everyone is being seen clearly and that lighting cues are accurate. Set directors want to make sure that the sets and props are in working order. No one wants to see an actor close a door on the set and have the set come tumbling down—unless that is what was intended. During these rehearsals, technical adjustments will be made, which will prolong the rehearsal. Tell everyone to prepare to be there a while. When major technical changes need to be made, they should be discussed when first discovered, but then worked on after the rehearsal has ended and the actors have left. Generally, you don't want to stop rehearsals for more than five or ten minutes, at the most.

Dress Rehearsals

Dress rehearsals take place when all the elements come together, typically beginning a few days before opening night, or prior to your previews if you are having previews. Actors will be in full costume and makeup, technical details will be in place, cues will be ready to be followed, and so on. Of course, during the first dress rehearsal, plenty of things can, and do, go wrong. This can be because actors and crew members are trying very hard to get everything just right, and there is a heightened level of tension. For this reason, producers and directors need to have patience and not panic. Try to work through all sorts of problem areas and keep everything on track. By the second dress rehearsal, each of the many initial difficulties will have disappeared and things will normally go much more smoothly. By the third, and in some cases fourth, dress rehearsals, everything should be running like clockwork.

Prior to dress rehearsals, everyone must know their preshow routine, which includes a sound check, lighting check, placing props on prop tables, and so on. Everything is treated as if it was a performance: cast members must be on time so they can have hair and makeup done and get into costume. If something is missing— I've seen situations where part of the set was not complete or was unavailable for some reason—the rehearsals should go on as planned. Even in previews such problems should not stop the show from moving forward. By opening night, however, everything must be in place.

Following a dress rehearsal, crew members shut down all equipment as they would do following a performance and make sure everything that needs to be stored is put away safely. A meeting of the technical crew is called so that they can review any problems that may have occurred. Likewise, the cast go to their dressing rooms to change out of their costumes and take off their makeup before meeting with the director to discuss the rehearsal.

Rehearsal Schedule

A sample schedule follows for the two months preceding the opening night of my show *In the Wings* at the Promenade Theater in New

York City. The schedule is very tight, and although it does not mention them by name, includes line rehearsals, tech rehearsals, run-throughs, and dress rehearsals for the final few days prior to the previews. Actors' Equity Association (AEA), the union for professional actors, requires one day off for six work days, which is why the off days are indicated as such. You will also notice that we included nearly three weeks of previews in which to hone the show in front of audiences.

August 2005

WEEK 1	Monday	Cast called for 10 A.M. for AEA business. 10:45 Meet & Greet
	Tuesday	Rehearsal 10 A.M. to 6 or 6:30 P.M.
	Wednesday	Rehearsal 10 A.M. to 6 or 6:30 P.M.
	Thursday	Rehearsal 10 A.M. to 6 or 6:30 P.M.
	Friday	AEA Day Off
	Saturday	Rehearsal 10 A.M. to 6 or 6:30 P.M.
	Sunday	Rehearsal 10 A.M. to 6 or 6:30 P.M.
WEEK 2	Monday	Rehearsal 10 A.M. to 6 or 6:30 P.M.
	Tuesday	Rehearsal 10 A.M. to 6 or 6:30 P.M.
	Wednesday	Rehearsal 10 A.M. to 6 or 6:30 P.M.
	Thursday	Rehearsal 10 A.M. to 6 or 6:30 P.M.
	Friday	AEA Day Off
	Saturday	Rehearsal 10 A.M. to 6 or 6:30 P.M.
	Sunday	Rehearsal 10 A.M. to 6 or 6:30 P.M.
WEEK 3	Monday	Rehearsal 10 A.M. to 6 or 6:30 P.M.
	Tuesday	Rehearsal 10 A.M. to 6 or 6:30 P.M.
	Wednesday	Rehearsal 10 A.M. to 6 or 6:30 P.M.
	Thursday	Rehearsal 10 A.M. to 6 or 6:30 P.M.
	Friday	Cast moves to rehearsal studios. Span of day: TBA, Load-in begins at Promenade
	Saturday	AEA Day Off, Load-in continues
	Sunday	Cast: rehearsal span of day TBA, Load-in continues at Promenade

AUGUST *continued*

WEEK 4

Monday	Rehearsal: Time TBA, 7 or 8 out of 8.5-day for cast, Load-in continues
Tuesday	Rehearsal: Time TBA, 7 or 8 out of 8.5-day for cast, Load-in continues
Wednesday	Rehearsal: Time TBA, 7 or 8 out of 8.5-day for cast, Load-in continues

SEPTEMBER

WEEK 4

Thursday	Rehearsal: Time TBA, 7 or 8 out of 8.5-day for cast, Load-in continues
Friday	AEA Day off, Load-in continues
Saturday	Cast returns to Promenade, work-light rehearsal. Some sound 10 A.M. to 6 or 6:30 P.M.
Sunday	First 10 out of 11.5-hour tech day, Cast called at noon

WEEK 5

Monday	Morning work notes. Cast called at noon for 2nd 10 out of 11.5-hour tech day
Tuesday	Morning work notes. Cast called at noon for 7 out of 8.5-hour tech day
Wednesday	Morning work notes. Cast called at noon for 10 out of 11.5-hour tech day
Thursday	Morning work notes. Cast called at noon for 7 out of 8.5-hour tech day
Friday	Daytime schedule TBA. First preview 8 P.M.
Saturday	Morning TBA, rehearsal 2 to 6 P.M., preview 8 P.M.
Sunday	3 pm preview, possible note session

WEEK 6

Monday	AEA Day Off
Tuesday	Afternoon rehearsal TBA, preview 8 P.M.
Wednesday	Rehearsal 2 to 6 P.M., preview 8 P.M.
Thursday	Afternoon rehearsal TBA, preview 8 P.M., possible note session
Friday	Afternoon rehearsal TBA, preview 8 P.M., possible note session
Saturday	Previews, 2 P.M. and 8 P.M.
Sunday	3 P.M. preview, possible note session

SEPTEMBER *continued*

WEEK 7	Monday	AEA Day Off
	Tuesday	Afternoon rehearsal TBA, preview 8 P.M., possible note session
	Wednesday	Previews, 2 P.M. and 8 P.M.
	Thursday	Afternoon rehearsal TBA, preview 8 P.M., possible note session
	Friday	Afternoon rehearsal TBA, preview 8 P.M., possible note session
	Saturday	Previews, 2 P.M. and 8 P.M.
	Sunday	3 pm preview, possible note session
WEEK 8	Monday	Afternoon rehearsal TBA, preview 8 P.M., possible note session
	Tuesday	Afternoon rehearsal TBA, preview 8 P.M., possible note session
	Wednesday	Afternoon rehearsal TBA, OPENING NIGHT!!
	Thursday	AEA Day Off
	Friday	Daytime—day of rest: Performance 8 P.M.

Previews

Once you get to previews, you should be focusing your attention on the audience. Any theatre person will tell you that all the work you do, all the sweating and decision making, the ingenious set design, all the acting, and all the choices you have made up to that point do not mean anything until you get the audience in front of you. I can't stress enough how important previews are to gauging the results of all that hard work. Up until that point it's all guesswork. The actors are relying on the director and, while you may think it is good, you are still relying on your instincts. "I think it's funny but will they?" remains an unanswered question until the audience is in the theatre. With previews, the audience becomes part of the creative process. Ignoring the response of an audience is an exercise in self-indulgence, since plays are meant to be performed in front of other people.

In regional theatre, you may see preview nights on a Wednesday and Thursday, with opening night on Friday. In a school or community-group setting, you may use the preview night to get a few family members and friends to come see the show at a discounted rate. *Hint:* Don't exhaust your family and friends because you will want them there for opening night. You might invite local merchants to come for half price or provide complimentary preview tickets for those with whom you bartered for services and ads in the program. Sometimes a high school will do a preview show for the local middle school students or another invited group. The preview provides you with a response to your work. You'll want to see if they get the gist of the play. Are they laughing at jokes? Enthralled by the action? Enjoying the dance numbers? Looking at their watches and yawning? Their responses and reactions are worthwhile.

While you may charge admission for previews, they are linked to the rehearsal process. Changes can still be made, since you haven't frozen the show yet—meaning that it is officially set for the scheduled run. Sometimes you will determine from the audience responses that a few quick changes need to be made, or you will see some technical matters that can be altered, such as shadows on part of the stage, or microphones not picking up the vocals of a performer as well as they need to. In some cases, a more radical change is called for, such as when a show is running close to three hours and the audience is fidgeting in their seats. This may be the time to simply cut the show down to two and a half hours.

The more previews the better, because they provide a greater opportunity to watch and listen to the responses of various audiences. One Broadway show relied heavily on audience reaction and went from a struggling production to a big hit during the previews. At the Broadway level, timing is very important, and the availability of talent and a theatre that is right for the size of the show are vital. When we were working on *The Will Rogers Follies* in 1991, we did not have time to take the show on a tour to other cities (which is frequently done to iron out the kinks) prior to bringing it to Broadway. So, under the supporting gaze of the theatre community and the press, we bravely—and possibly foolheardily—started previews on Broadway on April 1. Within a week, articles in the newspaper declared the show was in trouble and said people were walking out during the performance. There were complaints that you could not see from the second balcony and general concerns about the show. Even *The New York Times* jumped on the bandwagon.

One thing we had learned over the years was just to keep on doing your work. Previews are a time to make changes; you have to ignore all the clamor, the clanging and the sirens out there and just stick to your job. This is exactly what Tommy Tune, our director, did. He kept on moving forward. When we'd see that something wasn't working, we'd try something else. We made numerous changes and steered clear of the press. By the second week of previews, fewer people were walking out, and by the third week, people were standing and applauding. By opening night we were a hit! We worked it all out through the previews. Not that you want to undergo such a transformation with all eyes on you, but a lot can be done during previews to turn a show around. So get as many previews as you can, and try to keep the media (or the principal or anyone else from whom you may hear criticism) from coming to your previews. Go by the audience's reactions and by your own reactions to the show before you.

There are some terms you should know if you are directing. Tell your actors to become familiar with these terms; they are part of the onstage language of the theatre. As a producer, you also want to be familiar with the lingo.

Cross—To have someone move from one area to another

Cover—To block the audience's view of a person or object

Closed Turn—To turn your back to the audience

Open Turn—To turn toward the audience

Full Front—To face the audience straight on

Open Up—To turn more fully toward the audience

Move On—To enter the stage ("Move on from up left")

Move Off—To leave the stage

Give Stage—To move to a less obvious position onstage

Take Stage—To move to a more prominent position onstage

Using the language of the theatre is a marvelous way to make even the newest of theatre newcomers feel that he or she is part of the theatre experience.

Marketing and Promotion

After opening night for *La Cage aux Folles* on Broadway, my father was reading the reviews. He sat there shaking his head, and he said referring to the review, "Look, he calls it an old-fashioned musical." I said, "That's a good thing, you're talking about calling a drag show an old-fashioned musical. That's good." He didn't buy it. In fact, he was so convinced that we had a flop on our hands that he persuaded me. That night, I was so despondent I drained all the Champagne bottles we had opened. The next day, I dragged my sorry body into the press meeting at the advertising agency, expecting to hear the worst. Everyone was dancing, overjoyed—the show was a huge hit and went on to win six Tony Awards including Best Musical. Needless to say, despite a mild hangover, I was thrilled, and also very thankful that my dad was not a theatre critic for *The New York Times*.

It has often been said that in the theatre there are three main elements: the play, the actors, and the audience. Thus far we've talked about selecting a play and auditioning and casting actors. We have only briefly addressed the audience in the previews. But it is the audience that completes the picture. They are the third piece of the puzzle and without them, you will never know for sure if your vision and all your efforts have been worthwhile.

Marketing and promotion are essentially very simple concepts: You want to spread the word about what you are selling, which in this case is a theatrical production and tickets to see the production, and, through various means, you want to reach as many potential ticket buyers as possible. This, however, is where the simplicity of the idea ends. In today's culture, with an astonishing number of stimuli all competing for our attention, "spreading the word" has become a science. Directors of audience development; media consultants; demographics experts; and advertising, marketing, and audience research firms are all involved in the process of analyzing the market for any given product. The key is to find the most cost-effective means of reaching your desired target audience and enticing them to purchase your product. At every production level, whether amateur or professional, promotion and marketing play an integral role in your success.

Since marketing materials take time to develop, do not wait until the last minute to get started. As soon as you know which show you will be staging, get someone on the job and have them begin creating a promotional plan, detailing who they are trying to reach and how they will attempt to reach them. Have people start on posters, press releases, and any other type of marketing and promotion materials you plan to use. Too many empty seats are the unfortunate result of waiting until the last minute to think about this part of the process, and it's extremely disheartening to hear people say, "I would have seen that show if only I had known about it."

The Publicity Process Begins: Determining Your Demographics

Like any good marketer, you need to take some time to figure out who are the most likely candidates to buy tickets to your production. A broad view of the show and the cast will usually give you a fairly good idea of whom it should most appeal to. The musical *Princesses* is set in a school for girls and includes more than a dozen teenage girls in the cast. It is ideally suited to young teen girls who are the age of those in the show—the nine- to fourteen-year-olds—with fringe audience groups of younger kids as well as high school and even college students, who can relate to some of the characters.

For any show, you will want to find this core audience. While it's nice to say that a show will appeal to "everyone," most shows, like movies, books, and music, have a specific group that are the "core" audience, or your target audience.

In a school or university setting, you have a built-in core group that consists of the students; their parents, friends and families; and the faculty. While these people may or may not relate to the show itself, they will come because it's always fun to watch people you know perform onstage.

Even in this type of structured community, though, you will still need to do some marketing and promote the show, especially if you are doing several shows and have a fairly large auditorium to fill. While you want to reach the entire student body, you also want to make a point of reaching specific subgroups who might be interested in your choice of musical or play. Your show may deal with alternative lifestyles, feature a specific ethnic group, or focus on an environmental or political cause of importance to a segment of the school or community. Make sure they find out about the show. Sometimes the show will feature a topic of interest to a particular group of students; for example, a work of Shakespeare will interest the Shakespeare club in the school. Make sure posters or fliers are seen by this prospective audience. You might ask the club leader if you can speak briefly about the upcoming show at a meeting. Dance students will likely have an interest in a Bob Fosse show such as *Chicago* or *Dancin'* or anything from a well-known choreographer. Don't assume that by putting up posters or announcing a show on the school radio station you will have reached enough ticket buyers.

The same holds true in all marketing. For children's theatre, reach out to nearby schools, after-school centers, and places frequented by parents of young children, such as local playgrounds, a neighborhood children's museum, or the local supermarket. Signs or posters in store windows are always a great ways to attract local interest. While store windows in general will attract passersby, you can target specific stores. A poster for your forthcoming production of *Cinderella* will fit nicely in a neighborhood toy store window.

Marketing for theatre has grown by leaps and bounds over the past thirty years. Not until Stuart Ostrow broke through with television advertising for *Pippin* were television and radio used to promote theatre. Newspaper reviews were essentially the means by which audience members learned about a show and whether it had merit. Advertisements in *The New York Times*, theatre posters, and word of mouth were the only other common means of getting the word out about a Broadway show. Once that barrier was broken, theatre began to reach out to a broader audience.

Today, it is not uncommon to see and hear commercials for Broadway shows on television, radio, and the Internet. Demographics are used to put the right show on the right website or the right radio station to reach a target audience. Ads for the show *Movin' Out*, featuring the music of Billy Joel and the dancing of Twyla Tharp, were more often heard on pop music stations than on the traditional classical or business stations. And you are more likely to catch a television commercial for Disney's *The Lion King* during an 8 P.M. family show than during a 10 o'clock program with a parental advisory. Similarly, popular websites with teen appeal are more likely to attract audience members for *Princesses*.

Think about whom your show will most appeal to and come up with your prime, core, or target audience. Then figure out the best ways to reach them.

The Promotion Should Match the Show

Earlier in this book I spoke about the Kaufman and Hart comedy *The Man Who Came to Dinner* and recalled seeing a poster for a rendition of the show featuring just a picture of the man in his wheelchair. Rather than appearing as a comedy, the poster looked like an ad for a charity—or at best a much more serious, dramatic play. The poster did not accurately represent the hit show. Unfortunately, it was certainly not the first time a well-intentioned advertisement misrepresented a show, and surely not the last.

I mention this as an example of how your promotion can mislead people and possibly leave you with empty seats. Design posters, flyers, and all advertising and promotional material with the overall theme of the show in mind. How should the show make your audience feel? Is it a cheerful musical romp? a farcical comedy? Is it an intense dramatic piece? Does the show deal with an important social or cultural issue? Is it provocative? outrageous? Whatever the theme and tone of the show, it should be reflected in your advertising and promotional materials and indicate whether you are promoting an upbeat musical or a serious drama. Everyone should immediately be able to distinguish a poster for *How to Succeed in Business Without Really Trying* from one for *Death of a Salesman* without reading a word.

Millions, if not billions, of dollars are spent annually on market surveys and focus groups to determine everything from the right look for a billboard to the right color for a can of soda. What will appeal most to the audience? is the question all marketers are trying to answer. Don't be afraid to do some marketing surveys of your own. Ask for feedback on designs, ad copy, colors, even the right wording. You want everything to properly reflect the tone of the show.

Prior to a reading for the musical *Princesses*, I put several posters in the studio lobby and asked people to vote for their favorite. This was a way of finding out which posters the audience felt best represented the show. People have surprisingly varied interpretations of the same piece of advertising. Along with generating valuable feedback, such marketing surveys allow people to feel they are part of the process. When people are a part of something, they are more likely to return and see it again—and send their friends to see it as well.

Hint: If you are performing a show in a school or for a religious or community group, or even for a business, make sure to run all promotional and marketing materials past the "higher-ups" before sending them out. Stories abound of offended parents complaining about a poster they saw for the school's upcoming musical.

Promoting a Season

A regional theatre company or a community theatre group putting on several shows in the course of a season requires marketing the broader concept that the community should come out to support the theatre frequently. The goal is to sell advance tickets and subscription plans. In fact, even a high school performing two shows in the course of the year could try using such a plan, whereby patrons could buy discounted tickets for both shows.

It may be beneficial for your theatre company (especially if newly formed) to start out with a common theme, using plays that will help define it; for instance, the works of Tennessee Williams or American plays by American authors; patriotic shows such as *1776* and those of George M. Cohan; the classic works of Marlowe or Shakespeare; or perhaps even a week of classic comedies. You might promote a new playwrights festival featuring original works by local talent. Focusing on a specific genre can help with marketing because you can shape your promotional materials to match the theme and target a more specific audience.

As long as you are not underpricing your tickets (and losing money), you can also come up with various discount plans that encourage people to buy tickets for more than one show. Or you might have a plan, even for a one-week run where you do not have a large advance sale, for all ticket holders to come back and see the show a second time for half price. This not only puts more people in the seats, but it gives you another opportunity to promote the next show to these audience members.

One of the keys to promoting a season's worth of shows is establishing a relationship with customers that ensures return business. In most industries, 80 percent of business comes from return customers, so it is beneficial to build such relationships in addition to marketing to new customers. Generating a mailing list (and an emailing list) can be extremely helpful, allowing you to send flyers, postcards, and other promotional material to your customers as upcoming shows approach. Entice people to sign up for your mailings.

Low-Cost Promotional Ideas

Advertising and promoting a show is thought to be an expensive undertaking. But it doesn't have to be. Short of advertising on television or placing ads in *The New York Times* or *Washington Post*, you can spread the word without spending a fortune. Here are some ideas:

Posters

Theatre posters have long been a staple in advertising upcoming shows. You can purchase the original theatre poster for the Broadway version of Alain Boublil and Claude-Michel Schonberg's *Les Misérables* for $86 from eBay, courtesy of Applause Broadway Theatre Posters, or, for just shy of $150, you can put a poster of John Guare's *Six Degrees of Separation* on your wall. Broadway and London theatre posters have become fashionable décor as well as valuable commodities in the collectibles market. However, the original intent of these, and countless other theatre posters, was to draw attention to an upcoming performance or run of a show. The theatre poster is one of the simplest and most creative means of attracting an audience. Look for someone with artistic talent and a flair for design and let them capture the essence of the show in a poster. If you can't find someone artistic, come up with someone who can print neatly and get the message across. Make sure to include all the pertinent details and be certain that the name of the show is clearly visible from a distance.

Handouts and Flyers

Both handouts and flyers are easy to create and print with software programs and color printers. Handouts do not have to be literally "handed out" but can be given to store owners to put in customer's bags in exchange for an ad in your program, or inserted into a school or local newspaper or Pennysaver or in the program for another local show or event. As long as you find ways to distribute handouts, you are accomplishing your goal.

Flyers should be a little more elaborate in their design. They can be left on tables in the library or posted on bulletin boards and other places where people gather—with permission, of course. You can also do a direct mailing if you have a mailing list. Flyers, or even postcards, can be effective, especially in an association or nonprofit group that can do a bulk mailing to the membership. (Prior to doing a bulk mailing, remember to check the postal rules, since bulk items are treated differently depending on how many times the piece is folded, whether it has staples, etc.)

Be careful not to pack too much information into your printed materials—remember, less is more. People need to be able to easily discern the name of the show, time and place, and price of tickets. If you can find a clever hook that fits the theme of the play and draws attention to your printed material, that can be a plus. If not, provide an eye-catching visual design and include only the necessary information. Always give potential ticket buyers a very simple means of purchasing tickets. If you leave a phone number to call and order tickets, make sure someone is manning the phone, or that all calls are returned promptly. One of the biggest mistakes made in direct mail marketing is not preparing people for the responses. Follow-through is vital to your success. If someone sees a poster and calls for tickets, and that call is not returned for a week, you have most likely lost that customer.

The Internet

The Internet is ripe with opportunities to advertise and promote a show. If you can afford to advertise on a popular website, you'll find it can be a marvelous way to reach your intended audience. Again, keep the ad simple and eye-catching, because it has to attract the attention of the viewer in about one second. The following are some places to consider when marketing your show.

Chat rooms: You can promote a show by beginning threads about it in local or subject-appropriate chat rooms.

Content: Many websites are constantly seeking content—as are online newsletters—and if you can write something that fits their content needs and touches on the subject of your show, you can contact the webmaster and gain some free publicity.

Web page: If your school or group has a Web page, make sure to get the show listed in some manner, with information about buying tickets. You can also have someone who is computer savvy build a Web page; it's easy to do.

Website: For a theatre company or touring theatrical group, it is essential to join the twenty-first century by having a website. Numerous books and articles offer details on how to build an impressive website for little money. The key is to promote your company and upcoming shows in a tasteful manner, with just enough photos and graphics to enhance but not overwhelm the site. Make sure the website is easy to navigate. Avoid bells and whistles and design your Web pages so that they can be easily viewed on smaller screens, such as a BlackBerry and notebook computers. Don't forget to post all contact information on each page and respond to email questions promptly. Also, make sure that all promotional and marketing materials have your URL (or the school's or association's) listed.

If you are able to sell tickets over your website, make the process easy to follow and have a system whereby you know immediately which seats are sold so that you do not duplicate sales.

Also remember to link your website to other appropriate sites. Linking is easy to do, and you can reciprocate by linking the other person's site. (Always look at their site before making this arrangement.)

Hint: Don't rely entirely on your computer for online sales information—make up a printed list. There are too many stories of people buying online tickets, only to find out that the transaction was lost somewhere in the process. Back up all ticket sales information (and all other information pertaining to the show) onto CDs, printed hard copies, or both.

Keep the site current. By updating your website with new content about the shows you are performing and news headlines, such as "25th Consecutive Sold-Out Performance!" you can draw people back to your site. You can also run special promotions or discounts. A clearly noticeable "forward to a friend" button can also prove beneficial; your audience will help spread the word about your theatre company. Using incentives also improves this word-of-mouth means of marketing—which is also called *viral marketing*. For example, let subscribers know that if they forward your information to a friend and that friend also subscribes to your theatre company, you'll give the original subscriber four extra tickets to a performance, or invitations to your upcoming theatre party, or whatever you feel is an enticing bonus that you can give without spending money.

Online listings: Groups working toward putting a production together can also surf the Net for local websites, which frequently have listings of area happenings. If you are part of a school or nonprofit group, these websites may include you on their listings for free.

E-newsletter: Theatre companies or groups that will be doing shows on an ongoing basis might also start an email newsletter featuring information on upcoming shows. Make sure to get permission to send to email addresses by having individuals sign up for the newsletter. Otherwise, you'll be sending spam, or unwanted email, and turning off potential customers (plus breaking the law).

In a newsletter, don't simply promote yourself or it will turn into an ad, which people are quick to delete. By providing some content, you can hook readers into looking at the newsletter—and even anticipating it. The concept is the same as buying a newspaper or watching a television show. Readers or viewers don't mind the advertisements if they receive something they enjoy watching or reading. Advertisements by themselves get boring.

Content in an online newsletter can be brief—two or three paragraphs or a top-ten list. It should be of interest to your audience and not self-indulgent. For example, if you are doing a revival of *Dracula*, you could write, "How To Get The Perfect Dracula Look for Halloween." Get a few tips from your makeup artist and write up a few sentences. You could also write up something funny that happened while putting together the show—people love backstage details.

The point is, an email newsletter can be an extremely effective means of marketing if you can get people to stop and look at it. Then surround your content with all your ads and promotional materials.

Radio

Radio stations are another marvelous place to get some mileage without much, if any, cost. Public service announcements (PSAs) are free. If you are putting on a show that stresses reading or education, you may be able to tie into a PSA. You can also give away some free tickets in a radio contest. The station gets listeners to stay tuned to "win free tickets," and you get some publicity.

Local talk shows are also a means of generating attention. If you can find a program that has regular guests, send a press release about your production to the show's producer with a note saying that you would love to have a guest from your show on their radio program. This will work more effectively if you can tie your show in to something happening in the news.

Building a Presence in the Community

Being known around town can be very beneficial for a theatre company, community theatre group, or, for that matter, anyone with an upcoming show. Align yourself with book and literary clubs where you can possibly speak or drop off flyers or handouts.

Find out about appearing at a local festival or fair with some of your actors in costume. A few people dressed up as cats, if that's the show you are doing, will definitely draw attention, even if they are simply strolling down a popular street in your area. It's a great way to sell tickets.

Perhaps you can make a deal with a local store or restaurant to have a couple of performers appear and do a song or two from your musical. Malls love to have free entertainment, it draws customers. Line up a few malls in your area and perform a couple of songs at each. Bring recorded music or possibly a person with a keyboard to handle the accompaniment.

Along with appearances, always be on the lookout for places to dispense handouts and hang posters in the community. Just make sure you are not breaking and local laws or ordinances.

Giveaway Items

If you are the only person at the local antique show handing out balloons with the name of your children's theatre company on them to the otherwise bored youngsters, you can be sure you will get the attention of every young child in that store. Inexpensive giveaways can be very helpful.

Getting in Print

If you plan to advertise in newspapers or magazines, plan early. Make sure ads are made up well in advance, especially for magazines, which have a lead time of two, three, or four months. If you cannot afford to advertise in the print media, send press releases in the hope that the editors will write a story about your upcoming show(s) or your repertory company. Press releases are designed to grab the attention of an editor quickly and give him or her a reason to write about your show or theatre company. Make sure to first locate the editor or editors most likely to write about theatre and the arts. Then assume that he or she is getting two hundred press releases that day. While this may be an exaggeration, the point is that editors and staff writers are besieged by press releases, so you need to make yours jump out at them. Think of an angle. Does your show tie in with something going on in the community? in the world? in the news? Are you doing something new and unique on stage? Is someone in the show well known in the community, or a celebrity? Anything that sets your upcoming show apart and makes it stand out could be the impetus for a press release heading and a subsequent story.

Once you have found an angle, lead with it in your headline and first two or three sentences. Then move into the meat and potatoes—the details of the show (the who, what, where, when and why). Finally, give a brief overview of who is putting on the show. A little bit about the cast or the company will round out the press release, which should run one page at best.

Hint: Don't use every superlative in the dictionary. Let the information sell them on your story. Overselling is amateurish. Editors are smart enough to appreciate a good story without your telling them that it is the greatest story ever told. Here is a sample press release:

Waiting for fame is hell.
Have a nice day!

IN THE WINGS

a new
comedy by
STEWART F. LANE

Bonnie Comley and Stellar Productions Int'l, inc. present IN THE WINGS a new comedy by Stewart F. Lane with Lisa Datz Josh Prince Marilyn Sokol Brian Henderson and Peter Scolari - Songs by Michael Garin - Set Design William Barclay - Costume Design Mattie Ullrich - Lighting Design Phil Monat - Sound Design Jill B C DuBoff - Production Manager PRF Productions - Production Stage Manager Pamela Edington - General Manager Roger Alan Gindi - Casting Liz Lewis & Elizabeth Bunnell - Press Representative Keith Sherman Assoc. - Marketing HHC Marketing - Directed by Jeremy Dobrish

CALL TELECHARGE.COM (212) 239-6200
Promenade Theatre 2162 Broadway (at West 76th St.) www.InTheWings.biz

August 11, 2005

FOR IMMEDIATE RELEASE
*Contact: Keith Sherman & Associates at
1.234.456.7890*

**BONNIE COMLEY AND STELLAR
PRODUCTIONS INT'L PRESENT**

LISA DATZ, JOSH PRINCE,
MARILYN SOKOL, BRIAN HENDERSON,
AND PETER SCOLARI

IN

**A NEW COMEDY BY
STEWART F. LANE**

DIRECTED BY JEREMY DOBRISH

IN THE WINGS

PERFORMANCES BEGIN FRIDAY, SEPTEMBER 9
AT THE PROMENADE THEATRE
OPENING NIGHT WEDNESDAY, SEPTEMBER 28

CALL TELECHARGE.COM (212) 239-6200

She's an actress . . .
. . . He's an actor.
She loves him . . .
. . . He loves her.
One is about to get a big break . . .
. . . One is about to get a broken heart.

Bonnie Comley and Stellar Productions Int'l present *IN THE WINGS*, a new comedy by three-time Tony Award–winner Stewart F. Lane at the Promenade Theatre (2162 Broadway at West 76th Street). Directed by Jeremy Dobrish (*Duet!, Maybe Baby It's You*), *IN THE WINGS* features Josh Prince (*Forbidden Broadway, Little Me*), Lisa Datz (*The Full Monty, Titanic*), Brian Henderson, Emmy and Obie Award–winning actress Marilyn Sokol (*Guilt Without Sex, Grease*) and Emmy nominee Peter Scolari (TV's "Newhart," Broadway's *Sly Fox* and *Hairspray*). Original songs are by Michael Garin (*Song of Singapore*). The scenic design is by William Barclay, costume design by Mattie Ullrich, lighting design by Phil Monat and sound design by Jill B. C. DuBoff.

Set in 1978, *IN THE WINGS* tells the story of Steve (he's Jewish) and Melinda (she's not), two aspiring actors in love with each other and the theatre. They get their big break when they are cast in a new musical, "I Married a Communist," written by their svengali-like acting teacher, Bernardo. But when the show moves to Broadway, only Melinda is asked to move with it. Can love stay alive on the Great White Way?

"After three Tony Awards, most people know me as a producer," says Lane, "but once upon a time, I struggled to make a living on the other side of the footlights. The life of an actor in this city was not an easy one, but those were some of the best years of my life. This particular time in my life seemed like an ideal foundation on which to create a romantic, New York comedy like *In the Wings.*"

IN THE WINGS, a romantic comedy by Stewart F. Lane and directed by Jeremy Dobrish, begins performances Friday, September 9, at Off-Broadway's Promenade Theatre (2162 Broadway at West 76th Street). Opening night is Wednesday, September 28. Performances are Tuesday through Saturday at 8:00 P.M. with matinees Wednesday and Saturday at 2:00 P.M., and Sunday at 3:00 P.M. Tickets are $66.25 for all performances. Tickets and information are available at Telecharge.com (212) 239-6200. Visit the official website at www.InTheWings.biz

You can also approach columnists who write about theatre and the arts with an idea that might fit into their column. Read columns and determine which columnists might be most interested in your show. Don't be afraid to utilize a technical angle if that will work. For example, a columnist who writes about fashion and beauty might be interested in what your costume designer has to say about the latest styles, or perhaps the return of styles, featured in your show. Be creative; free press can be marvelous.

Be prepared to follow up on any press releases sent out. This means that if someone does take an interest and want to do a story, you need to be ready and willing to do an interview. Have all contact information on the release and understand that while many press releases will fall into the circular file, those that do strike a chord will only hold that chord for a short time. Don't miss the opportunity to get into the press by telling a reporter you'll get back to them.

Hint: Stick to the topic when being interviewed. Don't veer off on tangents and don't run on endlessly about every little detail of the show, your career, or your childhood. Stay focused.

Tickets

While there is not much room to print anything besides the important information on a ticket (title, time, date of the show, row and seat, price) a promo for your next show squeezed onto the back of the ticket can serve as an additional means of promotion. Have all tickets numbered so you can keep track of exactly how many have been sold.

Quality Customer Service

While customer service is not a means of promoting the show or the theatre company, it can certainly play a role in your upcoming ticket sales. One of the hallmarks of any industry that deals with the public is the quality of service provided to customers. This carries over to the theatre. Your box office, including all means of sales, must be run efficiently and with professionalism. From inquiries about prices and the availability of tickets to customer complaints, everyone dealing with the public on behalf of your show or theatre company must be ready to try and solve problems in a courteous manner. The quality of service provided can put your audience in the right frame of mind to enjoy the performance and return for your next show. Conversely, disorganization, rude sales people, or any poor customer service can result in theatregoers who not only won't come to the show but are certain to spread a bad word about your production to their friends and families. This can be a painful way to lose credibility after working so hard on a production.

Complimentary Tickets (Comps)

Yes, you will be giving a certain number of tickets away to your show(s). Some will be as part of your barter deals, while others may be for teachers in your school, special guests, or members of the press. The problem is that too often complimentary tickets get out of hand. Limit from the start the number of complimentary tickets you will have per show, and make a rule that all requests for comps need to be okayed either by you or someone who can put up with that one person in every production who is always whining about needing more comps.

If you start out with a set policy (posted in writing), you can stick to it for everyone involved. Friends and relatives can afford to spend a few dollars to see your actors perform. In amateur productions, this is a large segment of the audience. It is how you raise money for a good cause or cover your expenses.

Also, make sure that anyone who is comped either has actual tickets in hand or is on the guest list for the show. It's very embarrassing to have the mayor, or another VIP, show up and be stopped at the door because nobody informed the box office that this person was on the guest list.

The Program

You may wonder how the program can help you promote your show, since the audience members receive it at the show. If you are having upcoming shows, this is the perfect place to promote them. This is also the place for selling subscription plans.

All theatres typically have a program of some sort. Whether printed professionally or on a home PC, the program should provide brief backgrounds on the cast and crew, the scene list, the songs (for a musical), possibly photos of the cast members, and a short background of the show if you are doing a revival. If you have any copies of a professional program or an old *Playbill* from a Broadway show, use it as a template. Remember to put in the advertisements for all your barter deals and, if you have room, list some local dining options in the neighborhood. This is a another means of connecting with the community.

In a volunteer situation, look for someone with layout experience to put the program together. Desktop publishing can produce quality programs, but you will need someone with the ability to give it a professional look. Have whomever you select to do your program stay aware of any changes in the production and ask for feedback about the look of the program before it goes to print. Also make sure they stick to the schedule, especially if working with an outside printer who will generally need at least a week to get the program back to you.

Finally, make sure the program is proofread carefully prior to sending it off to the printer and reviewed again when returned. Printers can make mistakes and it's very embarrassing to realize too late that you've just handed out two hundred programs for *Piddler on the Roof.*

Marketing and Promotion Can Pay Off

In the end, good marketing and promotional ideas and a well-executed plan from early on in the process can fill the house. And there's nothing like the energy and excitement of a packed house. Once unheard of, today's shows can survive even without the best of reviews. Reaching a target audience, creating a buzz about the show in the media, and spreading the word via the Internet, can continue to put people in the seats.

Of course, the longer a show runs, the more creative you will need to be when it comes to promotion. If the show is successful, with favorable reviews, you can start utilizing the press clippings as well as quotes and comments from audience members to market the show. Since word of mouth is a great means of promotion, television commercials for several Broadway musicals, such as *Cats* and *Les Misérables*, have featured young and old audience members talking about how much they loved the show. If you can't afford local television ads, use your website for the same purpose, putting up quotes from audience members and photos from the show to draw both new and repeat ticket buyers. Let the success of the show help you sell the show.

Also, don't stop writing up press releases. A new cast member, particularly one with a locally known name, will give you a new round of excitement about a show and possibly prompt a new newspaper story. Raquel Welch, Lauren Bacall, and Debbie Reynolds each brought us new publicity when they took over the lead role in the Broadway version of *Woman of the Year*. Always look for a new angle to put the show in front of the media. And look for new promotional ideas. If you're putting on a weeklong production of *Grease* in your high school, promote one night as a costume night and give a prize to the audience member with the best "Greaser" look. Be creative.

The audience is the missing variable when you are putting together a production. Remember that once the show is up and running, they become the most important factor, so don't stop promoting your show until the final curtain of the final night.

Reviews

No, reviews are obviously not part of your initial promotion and marketing campaign, since the show is not up yet. You can, however, use good reviews as a major tool in promoting an ongoing show or an upcoming season. In fact, your press kit and press releases should make it very clear that the show garnered positive reviews from the critics. Most newspaper critics won't review an amateur production, which is usually a positive, since the last thing a volunteer needs is hurt feelings and diminished confidence from a bad review. Regional theatre, however, can benefit from positive reviews when it comes to building a subscription base. Actors in summer stock can also use positive reviews for their personal bios.

Promotion notwithstanding, everyone has their own individual approach to reviews. Some actors never read them. Their spouse or friends might give them the highlights, but they still do not read the reviews, assuming, and rightfully so, that since they are finding regular work, that they must be doing something right. Other performers pour themselves a stiff drink before daring to read a review. As a producer, the best you can do is remind your players that it is only one person's opinion and that they should not take it to heart, even if, deep down inside, your stomach is churning.

I was always one of those producers who couldn't wait for the reviews to come out. Forget the opening night party; I would be at the advertising agency waiting for the guy who worked in the printing room to read me the headline of the review before it hit the stands. I lived and died by the reviews.

One of the first shows I did was *The Grand Tour*, the 1979 musical version, with the book by Michael Stewart and Mark Bramble. We got three or four Tony nominations, but the show closed after just three weeks and I was devastated. I thought I'd never work in this town again; no one would ever want to produce a show with me. I was so upset over *The Grand Tour* not working that when I was offered another show, I turned it down. The show was Ralph G. Allen and Harry Rigby's *Sugar Babies*, which of course became a big hit. In time I learned that it was all part of the business. For every producer, director, and performer, there are a few disasters along the way. Even Spielberg had his *1941*.

When Broadway was in its heyday in the 1920s, theatres were booked solid with entertainment, from Eugene O'Neill to Olson and Johnson's *Hellzapoppin'*. New York had thirty newspapers—and those were just the ones in English. Over time, the number of newspapers in town dropped drastically and, with relentlessly decreasing media exposure, the words of a handful of critics began to mean life or death for a Broadway show. As a result, critics wielded great power and, since theatre was considered a rather "sophisticated" art form, an elitist point of view emerged.

Unfortunately such a view did not allow for a wide range of creative ideas to be seen. The ancient art form could not rejuvenate itself, nor did it reflect the community at large. As a result, theatre struggled for many years. The small niche audience was unable to maintain very many shows; as a result, at any given time, a number of theatres would remain dark.

In time, more newspapers and other media forms began disseminating Broadway theatre reviews, and the opinions of a greater, and more diverse, group of critics were heard. Now, Broadway reaches a huge audience, and includes more young theatregoers than ever before. We are in a neo-golden age of Broadway.

It is still nearly impossible to survive consistent negative reviews, but if some of the critics are on your side, you stand a fighting change. Although Andrew Lloyd Webber, for example, has not been popular with some of the critics, when his shows, such as *Phantom of the Opera* come to town riding on their success in London, people are intrigued. The shows have a certain cachet, like an English pedigree. Even *Cats* was not well liked by some critics. Other shows, like *Beauty and the Beast*, did not win any major awards, but through the magic of Disney and plenty of promotion to their young audience, they have become huge hits. After all, how many nine- and ten-year-olds care about the opinion of a theatre critic anyway?

The point is that today, a show without stellar reviews can survive because there are so many different audiences that can be reached through television, radio, and the Internet. Never underestimate the importance of marketing and promoting your show.

Playwriting

An Overview

No matter what is written on the page, there are moments that can only happen in live theatre. It is these unscripted moments that remind you of how unique an art form theatre really is.

Although I had nothing to do with this particular show, this is a great story of how things do not always go as planned. The production was a community theatre version of *Miss Saigon*, the musical based on *Madame Butterfly*, being performed in Brooklyn. The show was quite good and was nearing the finale when the lead character pulled out a gun to shoot herself. On this particular night fate intervened and attempted to write a new ending to a most dramatic moment. When she pulled the trigger, the gun made no sound. Again she pulled the trigger, and again nothing. Once more, she pulled the trigger—nothing. Finally, she pulled the trigger one last time, and someone in the audience yelled out, "bang!" to which she fell to the stage in a heap.

While laughter is not the typical ending to this dramatic show, it was indeed a performance audience members would never forget.

This chapter takes a slight detour from the production end of theatre into an area that deserves some attention: playwriting. While
you may or may not be sitting down to try your hand at an original script, it is advantageous to understand the process by which
plays, including musicals, are created. You may also find, while
putting together the details of a show, that members of your cast
and crew will express an interest in writing a play. At some point
you may get the playwriting bug as well. At any rate, and for the
purposes of producing and directing, you can benefit from having
a clear idea of the basic playwriting process.

Prior to writing a script, it is important for a playwright to
ingest a variety of plays to understand how the finished product
looks, sounds, and moves. Seeing shows in various genres and reading scripts helps playwrights, actors, producers, and directors gain
greater insight into the many possibilities that sit before them. By
reading and watching plays, you learn how the play evolves from
the page to the stage. If you enjoy theatre as much as I do, you may
find yourself inspired to sit down at the computer keyboard and
start writing.

Check out playwriting courses at local universities or continuing education programs. Courses teach you how to develop a story,
how to develop characters, and how to use dialogue to move the
story along.

This chapter covers some of the basics. For anyone who is
ambitious and determined to write a play or learn more about the
process, there are many excellent books on the subject, including
Jean-Claude van Itallie's *The Playwright's Workbook*, which provides
tremendous hands-on material, Kenneth Thorpe Rowe's *Write That
Play*, which offers a full exploration of scene dynamics, and *Writing the Broadway Musical* by Aaron Frankel, a good read for those
with a penchant for creating a musical.

Playwriting 101

From a helicopter on stage in *Miss Saigon* to an ocean liner in Peter
Stone and Maury Yeston's *Titanic*, money, time, creativity, and imagination allow for infinite possibilities. You can do a Busby Berkeley
musical like *42nd Street* or have your leading characters fly across the
stage to delight young and old audiences alike, in *Peter Pan*. You can

do anything on stage, but you must keep in mind that theatre is a stylized form. The idea is to create an original piece that fits that format. For this reason, the director's interpretation of the written work will prove impressive if he or she can visualize, in many different ways, what is on the page.

In addition, theatre, unlike television and film, presents the opportunity for performers to touch audiences on a much more personal level, and the audience has the opportunity to use their imagination—something that is often lost in television and big-budget action films with everything spelled out for the viewer in no uncertain terms.

A playwright must be creative when setting up scenes and putting the audience in the time and place chosen for the story. Sure, a narrator can fill in all the details, but it is far more interesting to do so by using the setting and the dialogue. For example: A couple in their late fifties / early sixties sit side by side. He's holding a steering wheel and she's looking all around, very excited. She says, "I haven't been here since the protests of the late sixties, and then I was too busy getting arrested to notice what a beautiful city this is." To which he responds, "Yeah, I've always loved this city, but a lot has changed in forty years . . . like the Sears Tower; you used to be able to go to the top, but now they won't let you. Still, I'd retire here if it didn't get so damn cold in the winter."

Very simple, but from three sentences, we know that they are driving through Chicago, visiting, in current times, and that she is excited about their visit. We also know that she was once a bit of a rebel and that he has thoughts of retirement.

The point is, in theatre, a simple setting or a few lines of dialogue can put the characters anyplace in the world and at any point in time, without paying to have expensive aerial photography for establishing shots, as is typically done in film.

The Story

The most important element of writing a play is having a story with a beginning, a middle, and an end. The story may or may not be detailed from the start. Some playwrights have an elaborate story in mind, perhaps based on a personal experience or an event in history. They see many of the key elements that they will incorporate from the outset, all leading to their intended conclusion. Other playwrights start with two or three characters, a defined relationship between them, and an idea of where the play is going. Then let their characters lead them there. Playwrights sometimes call this the magnet approach, meaning they are pulled where they are ultimately headed as if by a magnet as the play unfolds. It's like someone who knows where he or she is going but is not quite sure which route will lead there.

Glenn Young, a professor of playwriting and the founding publisher of Applause Books, explains the artistic development as plot. "A dramatist's chief power, according to Aristotle, derives from his ability to 'arrange the incidents' of a plot in such a way that its mere re-telling compels an intelligent emotional response from the listener. Cleverness or glibness of dialogue or the oft praised 'ear for gab' are happy gifts for the raconteur at a dinner party but of little value to the serious dramatist. Charting the characters' fate along the lines of a play's central action and its attendant reversals and complications, shouldn't inhibit the writer's spontaneous creativity, but rather focus and challenge it into greatness. A detailed plot is not meant as a talmudic final word, any more than an architect's early sketch becomes a despotic commandment of the final structure."

It is often recommended that in pursuit of a story, playwrights work with what is most familiar—the most common path for the new playwright. For example, a young couple I knew were living together and both pursuing acting careers. When she was suddenly cast in a major show and he was not, things started to get rocky between them. She went on to win Tony awards while he floundered at a radio station job. Could their relationship survive such diverse career paths? Their conflict sparked the idea to write the show *In the Wings*.

Sometimes, although not very often, the concept for a show comes knocking on your door. In the case of *If It Was Easy*, a play I cowrote with theatre critic Ward Morehouse III, I literally had people coming to my door, and even sending me money, to produce a musical based on the life of Frank Sinatra. Shortly after his death, a number of people decided that his story should immediately be recounted on Broadway. The problem was that there was no script, no story line, no show—nothing to actually put on the stage. In the end, the clamor for a show about the legendary vocalist became the premise for the show *If It Was Easy.* You never really know where the inspiration for a story will come from.

Whether predetermined or emerging during the writing process, a good story will drive a play and, in theatre, the dialogue and acting will keep it on course. One similarity between theatrical scripts, screenplays, teleplays and novels, is their need to hold the interest of the audience, which typically requires introducing some degree of conflict that must be resolved. Conflict does not have to be a major battle between warring factions. It can be as simple as two young lovers trying to be together despite the opposition of their of their parents. Or a young lion cub who is heir to the throne, but has to contend with his evil uncle before he can get that which is rightfully his. Normally the structure of a play begins with the character or characters having a problem that evolves into a conflict. That conflict builds to a crisis, which leads to the dramatic climax, where everything comes to a head. The resolution can come in any form and may or may not be anticipated by the audience. As director or producer, you will see this structure again and again as you look at ways to build the dramatic arc.

Another description of conflict in theatrical terms is when someone wants something and an obstacle—which could be a person, several people, a situation, an ideology—prevents the person from getting what he (or she) is seeking.

There may be more than one conflict, and more than one story line. The most basic examples of conflict come from children's literature, where an evil witch, stepmother, or jealous king stands between the main characters and their quest for love, riches, nobility, or all of the above.

It is conflict that draws the audience in and (we hope) holds their attention. They want to find out how that conflict is resolved. Most often a time element is also involved, making it more pressing that the conflict be resolved before some terrible finality, be it death, prison, lost love, being turned into a beast forever, or the audience's simply getting bored and leaving. To build suspense, the playwright might raise the stakes as the play progresses, just like in a poker game. This is called rising conflict. The more difficult it becomes for the main character(s) to resolve the conflict, the more anxious the audience will become because they want to see how everything turns out. The playwright should present heightened obstacles along the way and raise the bar by presenting new conflicting expectations—all in an effort to enhance the dramatic impact of the play.

Outlining

When writing original plays, I start with outlines. I know what I wanted each scene to accomplish and how the first act should end. I also have the end of the play in sight, so I know where I am heading (although a few years later I changed the ending of *In the Wings*). To start, I map out the story in the outline and list the key points to make sure I got to each one. Of course, starting with an outline does not mean the story is going to end up following it to the letter. Playwrights often find as they write that the play begins to take on a life of its own, and that is when the play becomes exciting and when it can take the writer on a journey. An outline keeps a playwright from veering too far off course and serves as a reminder that each scene must advance the story or plot.

An outline can be a few dotted words or a detailed illustration of each scene. There is no one-size-fits-all outline; each playwright must choose the one that best allows him or her to present the story on paper.

Some playwrights find that using an outline handcuffs their creativity as the story grows. They prefer to start simply, with characters and an ending, and use the magnet approach to find their way to a satisfying conclusion. Again, there are no set-in-stone rules.

Characters

The characters are the backbone of a script. Each of them must have a reason to be involved in the plot; otherwise, they should not be included. Producers and, more significantly, directors, actors, and the audience must understand why each character exists. The playwright's job is to ready each character to step off the page. The director and the actors then extend a hand and lead the character into the real world of the stage.

Characters must be well defined by what they say and do, how they dress, and how they act. Main characters start off in one place and, through the course of the script's events, follow a journey that leads them to a different place—emotionally, spiritually, or physically—by the end of the play. An important relationship in a character's life can bring about such change or self-realization or self-actualization. This is called an arc—the character starts out in one place and transforms through the course of the play—having experienced something new, different, engaging, or tragic.

Most playwrights base characters roughly on people they know. It is easier to write about people who are familiar, with defined characteristics from which to draw. Many playwrights like to create snapshots (or bios) of their character, describing their personality, what is important to them, and what drives them. Remember, each character needs a reason for being included in the script.

Well-defined characters come with a background story. The playwright provides answers to questions about the character, such as, How old is the character? Where did he grow up? Where is she living now? What was the character's family situation like? brothers? sisters? one-parent household? Is he single? married? divorced? widowed? What was the socioeconomic background of the character's childhood? What about today? What does she do for a living? How does the character feel about her job? Is he very social? Outgoing or introverted? What about friends? hobbies? habits? Does the character drink, smoke, or take drugs? conservative or liberal by nature? What are his pet peeves? What are the character's dreams or goals? regrets? What was school like for this character?

Secondary characters do not require as much detail. But make them interesting, which can mean quirky, outrageous, or offbeat, or with some personality characteristic that the director and actor can bring to life and that the audience will notice.

Some playwrights prefer to let their characters develop as the story and action unfolds. This allows them to build their characters as they see different personality traits emerge. The process is akin to traveling light and picking up what you need along the way to your final destination.

Characters are altered several times before the finished product is presented to producers and directors. In the end, there should be at least one character that the audience likes, relates to, or feels empathy toward. Conversely, at least one character should make your audience angry or uncomfortable. The worst response a playwright, actor, or director can get from the audience regarding a main character is indifference. If the audience doesn't care about the character, they will very likely lose interest in the show. Main characters need to stir up some kind of emotional response.

Another significant aspect (which is often the basis for the story line) is the relationship between the characters. Their connection and subsequent interactions exist to create and build the story and the conflict. The script must clearly define these relationships. Who is in love with whom? Which characters are jealous of one another? Who despises whom? Who wants secretly to do away with one of the characters? Their feelings toward each other must come out onstage. Plays are typically about how characters interact with each other or, in the case of children's plays, they may be personified animals. Whatever they are, the interactions even in a one-person show are crucial.

Dialogue

Dialogue, unlike other forms of writing, mimics the manner in which people speak. Since most of us do not use proper grammar in our everyday speech, dialogue is often grammatically incorrect. Playwrights listen to dialects and even tape-record people talking to get a general feel for various speech patterns.

Like people encountered in everyday life, characters will typically have different manners of speaking. One character may be from a strict upbringing, where speaking correctly and using proper English was mandatory. A character who grew up in an urban setting will be more likely to use the common street slang. Henry Higgins has a far more eloquent manner of speech than does Eliza Doolittle when they first meet in *My Fair Lady*. Of course, all of that changes through his hard work.

Most dialogue is fairly succinct; after all, we typically converse with one another in brief sentences. The playwright tries to avoid long monologues unless it is a pertinent time in the story for someone to take a stand and make an important, perhaps climactic, speech.

Characters who sound as if they are actually speaking to one another rather than reciting passages are far more genuine and more easily transcend that invisible wall between the players and the audience. For that reason, playwrights should recite lines aloud to hear whether they sound natural or wordy and cumbersome. Lines need to be carefully honed as they are written, read, interpreted, and performed. The irony is that playwrights, scriptwriters, and even stand-up comedians put great effort into crafting their words that sound quite extemporaneous.

Subtext

One of the most challenging aspects of playwriting is writing the subtext, which is essentially what the characters are not saying. It can, for example, be very apparent to an audience that there is a romantic connection without anyone ever stating that one character is in love with the other. Henry Higgins quite clearly has an affection for Eliza Doolittle, despite his not verbalizing it. In Tennessee Williams' *Cat on a Hot Tin Roof*, it appears from early on that Brit may have a homosexual attraction to his football buddy, although it was obviously not brought out in the script. Actions, looks, and dialogue that can indicate character's unmentioned intentions and feelings. We see and hear subtext in messages every day. We are constantly drawing conclusions from people's intonations, expressions, and gestures. The story's subtext expands on that concept. Sometimes you can feel the tension between two characters from a simple casual conversation. The fact that characters are communicating unspoken messages to the audience makes the characters—and the story—more complex and more intriguing.

The fun of the subtext is that everyone gets to play with it. Playwrights often find it easier to go back and see if they can indicate certain information in a more interesting, subtle manner, rather than having the character come right out and say it. Audiences enjoy dissecting the subtext as they try to piece together the manner in which the protagonist will overcome the conflict in the story. And directors and actors must be able to pick up on the subtext of a show and play it just right, meaning it cannot be so underscored as to go unnoticed, or so blatant as to lose the subtlety.

Two-Act Plays

Modern full-length plays are usually divided into two acts. The first act should build the plot to a point that heightens the intensity and has the audience trying to figure out how the conflict will be resolved in the second act. The act should end with some impact—either a new bit of information that has emerged or perhaps a twist of fate that intensifies the conflict. Whether through dramatic dialogue or a major song-and-dance number, it is imperative that, at the intermission, the audience is intrigued and wants to come back for more.

Within two acts, a play can have several scenes, allowing the playwright to advance the story and helping the director and the cast as they move through the logical sequence of events. Ordinarily, scenes are defined by a shift in location or a passage of time. A brief pause in the show to change scenery signifies a change of scenes as well. Lights can be brought down, or one section of the stage illuminated while another is dark. The transition from one scene to another is less often the playwright's concern and more frequently in the hands of the director or producer to work out. Unlike film, where it is easy to include numerous scenes in one script, a play is limited by the manner in which the play shifts from scene to scene. You will not typically see "act 2, scene 27." If you do, the stage crew will likely want to kill the playwright.

Moving in and out of Scenes

A key to writing strong scenes and keeping them moving quickly forward is knowing where to jump in to a scene and where to get out. For example, if a big moment in the story takes place at a party, the scene does not have to begin with people showing up for the party. The action can commence with the party already underway and lead to the point that furthers the story. The party does not need to go on too long, either. In essence, the audience is the "fly on the wall," dropping in to and out of the scene at the point where pertinent information is given. The information may be presented through song and dance, dramatic dialogue, pantomime, singing puppets, or any number of creative ways.

Rewriting and Editing

When playwright Peter Stone was working on the musical *1776*, the producers came to him and told him it was too long and needed to be shortened. Stone, unsure what they wanted him to do to shorten it, said to the producers, "Instead of thirteen colonies, we'll make it twelve. Which colony do you want me to cut?"

While the playwright traditionally is not at liberty to change historical events—too drastically—editing and rewriting are a large part of the creative process and one that continues even past the staging of the play. For more than twenty-five years I've tinkered with and reworked *In the Wings*.

Rewriting is your key to success, and it is important to under-stand from day one that nobody sits down and writes a finished work from scratch. We see the end product of numerous rewrites on television, in film, and in theatre, so it is easy to become disillu-sioned and believe that a play will come out fully baked and ready to serve upon the first writing. Instead, it comes out like a newborn baby, requiring time, plenty of attention, and patience just so it can stand on its own, much less run.

The first drafts of play scripts, even those of very successful shows, would shock most readers. They are often awkward and clunky, with undeveloped characters and long passages that bore even the fictitious characters within. Reading a first draft is not unlike seeing the first blobs of paint on a canvas, that later turn out to be a brilliant work of art.

With each rewrite, it is important for the playwright to imag-ine himself or herself sitting in the audience, watching the play. If the playwright is bored, the audience will be bored. The playwright must ask himself, (or herself), "I love this long monologue, but would the audience love it?" It's critical to look at a script objectively, taking the occasional step back to see it as if for the first time.

Reference points are also vital. We all know more terminology about our areas of interest and our chosen subject matter than the general public. A playwright penning a show about a computer genius who is using terms like *motherboard* or *applet* should wonder whether the audience will understand such terms. In many cases, it is a matter of doing some test marketing, which can include asking friends and family members if they understand what's going on.

Exposition—Development—Resolution

When the manuscript is finished, the first part of the script will focus on exposition, or the introduction of the characters. This means introducing the lead character(s), and presenting their situation(s) and their problem(s).

The development of the story and characters comprises the middle of the play (usually the middle third). This is where the con-flict arises and grows, the plot twists and turns and builds, and the characters go through all sorts of emotional highs and lows while taking the audience along for the ride.

The resolution, the third part of the script, is where the story reaches a climax and a conclusion. This should be generated from the story and characters that are already presented. Ideally, the conclusion is not too obvious.

Length

Full-length plays typically run between 90 and 120 minutes, not including the intermission. That being said, the point is for the playwright to feel he or she has told the story while holding the attention of the audience. If a play can keep folks on the edge of their seats for three hours, then the show will simply run longer than the norm. Playwrights, producers, and directors all need to keep in mind, however, that thanks in part to television, music videos, and the Internet, the average attention span of most audience members leans toward the shorter side of the spectrum, especially when presenting a play for young children. While there are some people who will sit through the full eight-and-a-half-hour version of playwright David Edger's adaptation of Charles Dickens' *Nicholas Nickelby*, it is usually asking a lot of an audience to sit for two and a half hours to three hours, even including the intermission.

Writing a Musical

It is generally agreed that the modern musical started with Rodgers and Hammerstein's *Oklahoma!* in 1943. The show was groundbreaking because it had songs written specifically to move the story along. This was in contrast to other shows, which simply included the popular songs of the day or were staged as revues, such as *Anything Goes*, featuring the music of Cole Porter. The songs in *Oklahoma!* were character driven and furthered the plot. It set the standard for musicals for the next thirty years.

Creating a modern-day musical is, therefore, unique in that a portion of the story is given in song. The dialogue bridges the songs and carries the story line. Most musicals are a collaborative effort between the songwriter and the librettist. When working with a songwriter, or songwriting team (composer and lyricist), the playwright will want to explain why each song is integral to the show.

Directors, choreographers, and performers must also grasp the reason for the inclusion of each musical number.

In some cases a song will advance the story, while in other instances it presents the viewpoint of a character or provides background information about the character as part of the exposition. Each song needs a reason to be included—one that is integral to the show rather than serving as a musical interlude, unless the goal is to do a revue.

A musical requires the same basic structure as a play, which means a story, complete with exposition; story development; and a climax; as well as characters that the audience will like, hate, or feel some other emotional connection to.

Bookless Musicals

In the late 1960s and early 1970s, Broadway met the "bookless" musicals. These were musicals that did not have a story but rather, tried to create an experience, such as the counterculture, tribal, rock musical *Hair*, by Michael Butler, which was a window into the hippie generation of the late 1960s, or *A Chorus Line*, which took the audience to an audition to meet the dancers, or even *Cats*, which was based on a collection of poems about felines by T. S. Eliot.

As is often the case, art comes full circle, and that has happened, in part, with some recent Broadway musicals. Not unlike the pre-*Oklahoma!* shows of the 1920s featuring contemporary hits of the day, several shows, including *Mamma Mia*, featuring the music of ABBA; *Jersey Boys*, featuring the music of the Four Seasons; and *Hot Feet*, featuring the music of Earth, Wind & Fire have utilized the same concept. These shows have loosely written story lines that thread together the music of the popular artists. Writing such a show means having an agreement with the songwriters to include the popular songs and then building a story line that allows the playwright to feature the popular music.

Get It Read

Remember, writing a play involves others. Actors will perform it and a director will help bridge the gap between what you have on paper and what takes place on stage. It is to the playwright's benefit to find workshops, classes, or stage readings in which to hear the play. Feedback at readings can prove invaluable. Some critiques will be on target, while others will be dismissed. Either way, feedback is always worthwhile, and playwrights need to try not to take it personally if someone does not love their work.

While a play is written to be heard, it should also be easy to read. Producers, directors, performers, or anyone else reading it should be able to focus on the play and not be thrown off by an unfamiliar format.

Nuts and Bolts: Structuring the Manuscript

Just as theatre is a diverse form of expression, the manner in which plays are presented on paper varies somewhat, depending on whom you listen to. The key is to format it so that it is easy to read and consistent throughout. Playwrights can purchase any of several scriptwriting software programs that help with the format by providing adjustable templates.

Some basic formatting principles include:

- Use standard white 8.5-by-11-inch paper.
- Your left margin should be 1.5 inches.
- Your right margin should be 1.0 inch.
- Top and bottom margins should be 1.0 inch.
- Number your pages staring after the cast pages.

Have a title page: The title page should include the title of the script, name of the playwright, and contact information. Sometimes the number of draft is also included. Some playwrights add the date, while others do not.

Have a cast page: Following the title page is typically a cast page, providing a list of characters with a brief description of each. This can be straightforward, with simple descriptions, or you can include descriptions with some creative flair.

Have a song list: A musical should include a page listing the songs for each act and indicating which character, or characters, will sing them.

Act 1 / Scene 1: To begin, the act and scene are listed in capitals, centered, on top of the first page. Acts and scenes are both numbered. Acts are typically in Roman numerals, while scenes are not. They can be listed horizontally as ACT I SCENE 1 or vertically:

ACT II

SCENE 3

Setting the stage: Next comes the setting, which can be simple or complex, depending on how much scenery will be onstage and how the first scene is orchestrated. At the start of the scene, called "The Rise" (based on the curtain rising) and at the beginning of each act, the scene description is written starting 3 to 3¼ inches in from the left margin and extending to the right margin. Each new scene sets up a change in time or place, which can be indicated in the setting description along with the location. Some playwrights provide more detailed descriptions than others. This can depend on how much the specific details matter to the scene. For example, one script will say, *A tastefully modern living room.* Another script may mention a modern sofa, wooden coffee table, end tables, hanging lamps, and so on. If the objects do not come into use during the scene, it may be best if the playwright is not overly descriptive, allowing the director to interpret the work in various ways. But the script should provide a fairly complete picture of what that room or location looks like.

The script should also be precise as to where the characters should be, for the sake of the director and the readers. Familiar stage terms, such as *down* or *up*, short for *downstage* or *upstage*, should be included. If not, the director should add them to the scripts before handing them out to the performers. Because stages were once built on a slant the back part of the stage is *upstage*, which was literally "up," while *downstage* refers to the front of the stage, which at one time was "down."

The dialogue: Once the stage is set, literally, the dialogue begins, with the character's name in capital letters and the dialogue starting at the left margin and continuing across from margin to margin, single spaced. Basic stage directions for characters' actions are included in parentheses. The character's name should always be capitalized and set 2½ inches from the left margin.

Other fine points regarding structure are available in books and on websites devoted to playwriting. Software products can handle much of this formatting, allowing the playwright to focus on the most important aspects of the play: the story and the characters.

Stage directions, are best kept to a minimum in the script. The director and actors need only know about actions or movements necessary to the story. For example, if a character is to show up carrying a very large package, that needs to be included. When mentioning a character in the stage directions, the names can be capitalized or not. For example:

> DEAN
> Well, I'd love to stay longer, but I have an execution to perform in the morning and I hate to have that sleepy feeling for a beheading . . . you don't want to screw up, you know.

> (*Dean gets up, kisses Melinda, nods to Merlin, and exits through the front door.*)

> Or:

> (*DEAN gets up, kisses MELINDA, nods to MERLIN, and exits through the front door.*)

Note that the character's name is in caps, the dialogue runs from margin to margin and the stage directions are in parentheses, in this case highlighting the characters.

One-Act Plays

A one-act play is, as the name suggests, a play without an inter-mission, consisting of a single act. While such a play could last anywhere from ten to ninety minutes or more, the modern-day one-act play is typically short, running twenty or thirty minutes. For a new playwright, it is a way of testing the waters. The same principles that apply to a full-length play also apply to one-act plays. They still require a structure (a beginning, middle, and end), the development of characters, and a conflict that creates the dramatic tension. All of this, however, is done with in a limited time frame. Several one-act plays, often featured in playwriting competitions, can provide an enjoyable night of theatre with diverse stories. Two or three one-acts—possibly on the same theme, such as patriotic plays for Independence Day or plays written specifically for Black History Month—can be educational as well as a good test for a new playwright. A shared setting can provide an interesting backdrop, since the individual plays utilize the same scenery in very different ways. *Hint*: Keep a one-act play simple in terms of set and costume changes as well as technical demands.

The Playwriting Mind-Set

There is no universal way to begin writing a play. For some, it commences with a very detailed story, while for others the process starts with a germ of an idea that grows. Writing has to be viewed as a process, a negative that slowly develops into a photograph. Each playwright needs to approach the process knowing that the initial script will be far from perfect, but will evolve over time. The playwright must have a vision and picture the action of the play as it unfolds in his or her imagination. Characters' voices, clothing, and the setting are part of this vision. As Glenn Young explains, "The playwright is the first and most lasting stage designer, costume designer, and lighting designer of the play. The environment and décor of a scene are critical leading players. They need to be thought out as carefully as the characters themselves."

This does not minimize the contributions of a creative team, but emphasizes the need for the creative team to work within the concepts and foundation of the playwright's vision. Young adds, "It does serve as a reminder that the more a playwright gives away in regard to creative control, the more he or she is giving up of his or her creative vision."

Conclusion

At a recent charity fundraiser for a not-for-profit theatre company, I unintentionally got into a heated conversation with a young woman sitting near me. She was claiming to be happy that she had not won any of the items auctioned off because they were too expensive and, after all, "this was not cancer research." I tried to explain that while cancer research keeps people alive, theatre provides meaning for their lives.

Humans are the only creatures aware of their own mortality, and theatre celebrates the human condition, with its tragic and comic foibles. Our need to commune and communicate is well documented, from prehistoric cave paintings to Japanese Noh drama. Theatre helps us give meaning to our existence, celebrates life, and helps us come to terms with death. In Thorton Wilder's play *Our Town*, the character Emily, who has just revisited an ordinary day in her life, turns to her guide and asks, "Do they [humans] ever know how wonderful it [life] is?" "Maybe saints and poets," he replies. As poets of the theatre, we try to explain the wonder of life. This expression spans continents, crosses religious and cultural barriers, and unites us all.

Numerous interpretations we give to a single theatrical work proves that theatre allows us to stretch our imagination. From schoolchildren to senior citizens, theatre touches all of us in very profound and distinct ways, providing each person with a unique experience, whether onstage, backstage, or in the audience. While science and medical research are invaluable, theatre has its place by providing a richness that drives the spirit and keeps our minds healthy and active.

All this is why I wrote the book, and perhaps to inspire others to become involved in the theatre. Wherever you go in America, you will find theatre companies. Professional, or amateur, profit or nonprofit, these groups help define their community and help us express ourselves as a nation. Why would you want to do anything else?

Resources

Websites of Interest

AisleSay.com: Index of national stage reviews and opinions from all around the United States.   www.aislesay.com

American Musical Theater Reference Library: Massive musical theatre reference portal.   www.americanmusicals.com

American Theater Web: The comprehensive site dedicated to American theatre includes listings of theatres, musicals, monologues, Broadway shows and theatre books.   www.americantheaterweb.com

Artslynx: Large portal featuring international resources dealing with all aspects of theatre and the arts.   www.artslynx.org

Broadwaystars.com: Provides numerous articles about theatre and the theatre community.   www.broadwaystars.com

Community Theater Green Room: Articles, how-to information, discussion boards, links, and scripts for community theatre. www.communitytheater.org

Curtain Rising.com: Link to more than eight thousand theatre websites throughout all fifty states.   www.curtainrising.com

CurtainUp.com: Reviews of numerous shows from everywhere. www.curtainup.com

The Costumer's Manifesto: Massive portal with links to help you find anything, from armor to wings.   www.costumes.org

Gilbert and Sullivan Archive: Courtesy of Boise State University, this is the home of the works of G and S plus lots more.   http://diamond.boisestate.edu/gas/index.html

Internet Theatre Bookshop: Volumes of plays, audition scripts, biographies of numerous theatre professionals and even gifts for thespians.   www.stageplays.com

Moonstruck Drama Bookstore: Long list of dramas and plenty of musicals available.   www.imagi-nation.com/moonstruck

Musicals101.com: An online encyclopedia of musical theatre and more.   www.musicals101.com

— **NYtheatre.com**: Listing of current plays, reviews, articles, ticket purchasing available.   www.nytheatre.com

Oscar Wilde Collection: His plays, plus poems and stories.   www.oscarwildecollection.com

Playwriting Opportunities: A site for playwrights with contests, competitions, workshops and more.   www.playwritingopportunities.com

Rosco International: A leading (but not inexpensive) place for lighting, gels, and other technical supplies.   www.rosco.com

Shakespeare, Complete Works: "The Tech," online newspaper from MIT, features the full Shakespeare catalogue. www.tech.mit.edu/Shakespeare/works.html

Talkin' Broadway: Broadway and Off-Broadway chat, theatre reviews, and more.   www.talkinbroadway.com

Theatre Development Fund: Discount tickets, education programs plus info on New York City theatre.   www.tdf.org

Theatre on a Shoestring: A comprehensive resource for producers working on a shoestring budget with links to numerous resources covering all production needs. www.upstagereview.com

Theatrecrafts.com: Growing portal with information on, and links to, useful technical information.   www.theatrecrafts.com

Theatre House, Inc.: Costumes, makeup, jewelry, wigs, masks, and much more for your stage needs.   www.theatrehouse.com

TheaterMania.com: A comprehensive resource for complete Broadway, Off-Broadway, and worldwide theatre listings, ticket discounts, news, and reviews.   www.theatermania.com

Tony Awards: Features information on nominees and winners of Broadway's most esteemed awards.   www.tonyawards.com

United States Copyright Office: For copywriting original works. www.copyright.gov

AND, I also invite you to find out more about my work at my website: www.mrbroadway.com

Theatrical Licensing Houses and Copyright

Applause Books and Cinema Books c/o Hal Leonard
A source for licensed material, the Hal Leonard Corporation is the world's largest music print publisher. For more than fifty years, they have been publishing and distributing publications and products for virtually every musical instrument. Also distributes sheet music through Music Direct.

PO Box 13819
Milwaukee, WI 53213
414-774-3630
www.halleonard.com

Bad Wolf Press
Numerous children's plays. "Musical plays for musically timid teachers."

5391 Spindrift Ct.
Camarillo, CA 93012
888-827-8661
www.badwolfpress.com

Baker's Plays
Full-length plays plus one-acts geared toward high school competitions as well as semiprofessional productions. Also, a variety of theatre books with up-to-date information to help you with your next production or audition.

PO Box 699222
Quincy, MA 02269-9222
617-745-0805 / Fax: 617-745-9891
Reading Room and Store
1445 Hancock Street
Quincy, MA
www.bakersplays.com

Dramatic Publishing Company
Numerous shows available from a longtime licensing and publishing company founded in 1885. Site features a Show Finder section to help with show selection, plus information about cutting or doing an adaptation of a show.

311 Washington St.
Woodstock, IL 60098-3308
800-448-7469 / Fax: 800-334-5302
www.dramaticpublishing.com

Dramatists Play Service, Inc.

Major house featuring an extensive list of titles, including a
preponderance of the most significant American plays of the
past fifty years.
440 Park Avenue South
New York, NY 10016
212-683-8960 / Fax 212-213-1539
www.dramatists.com

Music Theatre International (MTI)

The licensing home to thousands of scripts, featuring numerous
musicals designed for families and children including the Disney
collection. Also many shortened adaptations of well-known
shows for school productions.

545 Eighth Avenue
New York, NY 10018
212-868-6668 / Fax: 212-643-8465
www.mtimusicalworlds.com

Pioneer Drama Service, Inc.

Home to seven hundred plays designed primarily for educational
and amateur groups. Many short, entertaining plays geared for
young children.

PO Box 4267
Englewood, CO 80155-4267
303-779-4035 or 800-333-7262
www.pioneerdrama.com

The Rodgers and Hammerstein Organization

The R & H Organization represents numerous musicals and is
home to a Concert Library representing classic orchestral works
by great composers and songwriters, including Rodgers &
Hammerstein , Rodgers & Hart, Irving Berlin, Andrew Lloyd
Webber, Jerome Kern, Kurt Weill, and Cole Porter.

229 W. 28th Street, 11th Floor
New York, NY 10001
212-268-9300 / Fax: 212-268-1245
www.rnh.com

Samuel French, Inc.
Massive source of thousands of musicals and plays since 1830,
including numerous classics.

25 West 45th Street
New York, NY 10036
212-206-8990 / Fax: 212-206-1429
www.samuelfrench.com

Associations and Organizations

Actors' Equity Association
Founded in 1913, Actors' Equity Association is the labor union
that represents more than 45,000 Actors and Stage Managers in
the United States. Actors' Equity is a member of the AFL-CIO.
Regional offices in New York City, Los Angeles, Orlando, San
Francisco, and Chicago.

National Headquarters
165 West 46th Street
New York, NY 10036
212-869-8530 / Fax: 212-719-9815
www.actorsequity.org

Actors' Fund of America
A nonprofit, national human services organization helping
performing arts professionals in with various needs including
health issues and housing programs.
National Headquarters

729 Seventh Avenue, 10th floor
New York, NY 10019
212-221-7300
www.actorsfund.org

American Alliance of Theatre & Education (AATE)
AATE connects educators, artists, researchers, scholars, and
administrators, providing opportunities for members to learn
from each other.

7475 Wisconsin Avenue, Suite 300A
Bethesda, MD 20814
301-951-7977 / Fax: 301-968-0144 attn: AATE
M–F 9:00 A.M.–5:00 P.M.
www.aate.com

The American Association of Community Theatre (AACT)
National voice of community theatre, representing over seven
thousand theatres throughout the United States.
8402 BriarWood Cr.

Lago Vista, TX 78645
866-687-2228 or 512-267-0711 / Fax: 512-267-0712
www.aact.org

International Centre for Women Playwrights
Membership association dedicated to bringing international
attention to women playwrights, supporting their efforts, encouraging their works, and providing information.

Ohio State University
1430 Lincoln Tower
1800 Cannon Drive
Columbus, Ohio 43210-1230
www.internationalwomenplaywrights.org

National Alliance for Musical Theatre
A not-for-profit membership service organization that has been
dedicated to musical theatre for more than twenty years.

520 Eighth Avenue, Suite 301
New York, NY 10018
212-714-6668 / Fax 212 714 0469
www.namt.org

New Dramatists
The professional association of playwrights, composers, and
lyricists, since 1949.

424 West 44th Street
New York, New York 10036
212-757-6960 / Fax 212-265-4738
www.newdramatists.org

Books

The Art of the American Musical: Conversations with the Creators, by Jackson R. Bryer and Richard Allan Davison, editors. Rutgers University Press, 2005.

Broadway: The American Musical, by Michael Kantor and Laurence Maslon, Bulfinch, 2004.

Broadway Musicals: Show by Show, by Stanley Green. 5th ed. Hal Leonard Corporation, 1990.

Broadway Musicals: The 101 Greatest Shows of All Time, by Ken Bloom and Frank Vlastnik. Black Dog & Leventhal, 2004.

Directing Actors: Creating Memorable Performances for Film and Television, by Judith Weston. Michael Wiese Productions, 1999.

How to Audition for the Musical Theatre: A Step-By-Step Guide to Effective Preparation, by Donald Oliver. Smith & Kraus, 1995.

Light Fantastic: The Art and Design of Stage Lighting, by Max Keller, Johannes Weiss. Prestel, 1999.

The Musical: A Look at the American Musical Theater, by Richard Kislin. Applause Books, 2000.

On Singing Onstage, by David Craig. Applause Books, 2000.

The Perfect Stage Crew: The Complete Technical Guide for High School, College, and Community Theater, by John Kaluta. Illworth Press, 2004.

The Playwright's Workbook, by Jean-Claude van Itallie. Applause Books, 2000.

Scene Design and Stage Lighting, by W. Oren Parker, R. Craig Wolf, and Dick Block. Wadsworth, 2002.

The Season: A Candid Look at Broadway, by William Goldman. Limelight Editions, 2004.

Singing and Acting Handbook: Games and Exercises for the Performer, by Thomas Burgess. Routledge, 1999.

Stage Management Handbook, by Daniel A. Ionazzi. Betterway Books, 1992.

Technical Theater for Nontechnical People, by Drew Campbell. 2nd ed. Allworth Press, 2004.

Write That Play, by Kenneth Thorpe Rowe, Funk & Wagnalls, 1968.

Writing Musical Theater, by Allen Cohen and Steven L. Rosenhaus. Palgrave Macmillan, 2006.

Writing the Broadway Musical, by Aaron Frankel. Da Capo Press, 2000.

Magazines

American Theatre: From Theatre Communications Group, this monthly magazine offers the latest up-to-date information on the regional theatre scene and the not-for-profit theatre community. Online at www.tcg.org, click on *American Theatre*.

Back Stage: East and West Coast versions remain the leading source of casting news for actors. Also, reviews and news about the theatre community. Online at www.backstage.com

Playbill: For years, *Playbill* has been the name synonymous with theatre programs on Broadway. Now, they can also be found online at www.playbill.com.

Personal Favorites: Plays

Long Day's Journey into Night

The Iceman Cometh

Death of a Salesman

All My Sons

The Crucible

Inherit the Wind

A Streetcar Named Desire

The Glass Menagerie

The Cherry Orchard

The Three Sisters

The Heidi Chronicles

The Man Who Came to Dinner

Doubt

The Sunshine Boys

The Odd Couple

The Gin Game

Whose Life Is It Anyway?*

In the Wings**

If It Was Easy . . . **

*Play I produced
**Plays I wrote

Personal Favorites: Musicals

A Funny Thing Happened on the Way to the Forum

Fiddler on the Roof

My Fair Lady

Guys and Dolls

Rent

Chicago

Cabaret

Anything Goes

West Side Story

Oklahoma!

La Cage aux Folles*

The Will Rogers Follies*

Thoroughly Modern Millie*

*Shows I have produced

Index

Nederlander Theatre (New York, NY), 33
New Amsterdam Theatre (New York, NY), 33
New Jersey Shakespeare Festival, 3
New York Foundation for the Arts, 19
New York Screen Actors Guild, 19
New York Times, 48, 49, 108, 110, 113
Nicholas Nickelby, 139
'night Mother, 102
Nine, 33
1941, 126
noise, as consideration with sound effects, 45–46
Normal Heart, The, 5, 18–19
Norman, Marsha, 102
Northwestern University (Evanston, IL), 22

O'Brien, Richard, 15
Odd Couple, The, 39, 56
    female version, 87
    as taking place in one setting, 41
    timelessness of, 23
Oklahoma!
    casting, 87
    large space requirement, 16–17, 51
    as standard setting, 139
    timelessness of, 23
Oliver!, 15
Oliver Twist, 15
Olivier Award, 50, 74
Olson, John S., 126
O'Neill, Eugene, 15, 126
On the Town, 23
organizing the show. *See* getting organized
Oscars, 3
Ostrow, Stuart, 112–13
Our Town, 38, 145
outlines, in script development, 133
ownership in productions, providing, 25
Oz, 48

Palace Theatre (New York, NY), 1, 2, 14
Pal Joey, 64
Parabolic Aluminized Reflector (PAR) lamps, 44
Passion Fish, 3
Passion of Dracula, The, 39–40
patrons of the arts, 9–11

performance space, finding a, 48–59
    building and growing a show, 57
    profit, turning a, 52–54
    rental ads, reading the, 53–56
    theatre rentals, 50–51, 53–56
    touring, 58–59
    unconventional space, 56–57
performers, proper method of directing, 94–95
Performing Garage Theater Company, The, 17
Peter Pan, 8, 23, 129
Peters, Bernadette, 85
Phantom of the Opera, 127
Philadelphia Story, The, 93
Pioneer Drama Service, 22
Pippin, 112–13
Playbill, 124
plays
    children and. *See* children
    costs, 30
    ingesting variety of, importance of playwrights, 129
    musical or straight, deciding on, 20–21
    one-act plays, 143–44
    theatre needs, 51–52
    two-act plays, 136–37
Playwright's Workbook, The, 129
playwriting, 128–44
    bookless musicals, writing, 140
    characters, 133–35
    dialogue, 135, 142–43
    exposition, development, resolution in, 138–39
    getting it read, 140–41
    ingesting variety of, importance of playwrights, 129
    length, 139
    manuscript, structure of, 141–43
    mind-set, playwriting, 144
    musicals, writing, 139–40
    one-act plays, 143–44
    outlining, 133
    rewriting and editing, 137–39
    scenes, moving in and out of, 137
    the story, 129–33
    subtext, 136
    two-act plays, 136–37
plot, in script development, 131
political correctness, 20
politics, as hot button, 19–20

About the Author

A three-time Tony Award–winning producer, Stewart F. Lane's credits include more than twenty Broadway shows and numerous others in London, Ireland, and the U.S. Nominated eight times, he won Tonys for *Thoroughly Modern Millie*, *The Will Rogers Follies*, and *La Cage aux Folles*, and he has received two Drama Desk Awards, two Telly Awards, the Drama Critics Award, the Outer Critics Circle Award, and a Western Heritage Wrangler Award.

He has recently produced *The Two and Only* Off-Broadway and is currently producing *Legally Blonde—The Musical*.

Mr. Lane is the co-owner and operator of the Palace Theater in New York City, and he has also written two plays that were produced off-Broadway and regionally: *In the Wings* and *If It Was Easy*. He has also served for eleven years on the Board of Governors of the League of American Theatres and Producers. Stewart lives in New York City with his wife, Bonnie, and five children, Eliana, Harlyn, Leah, Leonard, and Franklin. Visit his website, www.mrbroadway.com.